Praise for
The Perfect Ofsted English Lesson

The debate about the perfect OFSTED lesson rages in schools up and down the country yet the need to rise above the formulaic and embed the quality learning experience for young people has never been greater. This welcome addition to the literature on school improvement, and that is what this book is, gives the reader the opportunity to enter David Didau's mind and classroom, and to see, smell and touch what outstanding learning is like when the competence and confidence of the teacher works in partnership with the curiosity and creativity of the student. The dashboard checklist to please the visitor who sits at the back of the classroom is relevant, but it is not the key to sustaining outstanding learning throughout a child's secondary education. The techniques and strategies that you will read in this book, drawn from the experiences of teachers David has worked with as well as those ideas that are his own, will help teachers of English reflect on what really matters when they teach the subject that has become along with Maths, the pivotal subjects in the curriculum for all school leaders.

David Carter, Executive Principal,
Cabot Learning Federation

The key to an outstanding English department is a relentless focus on the quality of teaching and learning. In this book David Didau offers a cornucopia of creative, practical and highly effective teaching and learning strategies. As a keen member of the #SOLOarmy, it's great to see a beginners guide to using the SOLO taxonomy, written in a clear, accessible style, with humour. As Head of English, I certainly will be purchasing a copy for each member of my department!

Rosanna Thorslund, Head of English,
St.Thomas More Catholic School, Blaydon Upon Tyne

The Perfect Ofsted English Lesson (or David's book) immediately gets to the heart of the learning. An essential read for all English teachers – not just to impress Ofsted inspectors! It is just as appealing and useful to dip into, as it is a thought-provoking read.

Bev Sharp, English Advanced Skills Teacher,
St Bede's Catholic College, Bristol

I have been in education for 26 years as a teacher, Head of Department, Senior Leader and Principal and have read many books regarding the practice of teaching. The very best of them offer practical advice on improving practice within the classroom that will directly impact on the learning of young people. This book does just that.

David Didau has produced a succinct, well structured and accessible piece of work that will be of use to beginning teachers and those who have taught for many years. Its great advantage is that it does not talk down to the reader, does not assume anything of the reader except one thing; that you are a teacher and therefore committed to improving your practice and to furthering pupil progress.

This book, although targeted towards English teachers, would also be of enormous use to any teacher. It lays out what an effective lesson looks like. It is deeply rooted in proven practice and Assessment for Learning and takes the reader through the key processes of lesson planning, lesson starters, learning objectives, pupil engagement, effective questioning and why the end of the lesson is as important as any other element. David explains the nature and reasoning behind formative assessment, peer and self assessment and the importance of knowing where the student is in their learning.

There are no fancy magic tricks in this book, there are no easy soundbites. Teaching is hard, David recognises this, but this book makes it easier to make an effective impact on students. Please don't be fooled by the title, this is no bow to Ofsted nor a clever way to fool them, this book is about teaching and how to do it properly. It is intriguing, engaging and that often overused phrase 'essential reading'.

If you are a teacher, not just an English teacher – you need to read this book.

Dave Rees Principal of Erne Integrated College

I've been a keen follower of David's 'Learning Spy' blog for some time now and so when I heard that he was going to write this book, I was very excited by the prospect, but also a little worried ...

Is there such a thing as a 'perfect' English lesson?

Well, I needn't have worried. If anyone could describe what makes a 'perfect' lesson, then it would have to be David. In this little gem of a book, David weaves the magic that will have even the toughest class under your spell whether you're an NQT or a little jaded and on the lookout for some new ideas.

He does all of this with charm and wit and a clear expectation that those things that are worth achieving need to be worked at – both by teacher and pupil. Uncovering the Holy Grail of pupil progress through SOLO Taxonomy along the way and giving some very useful and easy to implement practical tips. He also dispels some common myths about observed lessons and demonstrates that the best learning comes through collaboration, something that he is not afraid to do himself, drawing readily on the experience of others.

I'd recommend this book heartily to every teacher (NOT just English teachers) and encourage them to try out the tips within. They work ... I know ... I've tried many myself to great effect!

David Doherty, Assistant Principal and Teacher of English,
Cowes Enterprise College

Using his own love of teaching as fuel, Didau aims to reignite the enthusiasm of English teachers everywhere; his belief that every English lesson can be outstanding is inspiring. This book is an encouraging reminder that, with hard work, effort and an understanding of the fundamental pedagogies of our classrooms, we too can achieve perfection in our lessons. He provides English teachers with a wealth of ideas, techniques, hints and tips which have all been tried and tested in his own classroom. Being a current Head of English, he is well aware of the pressures which everyday teachers face. In short, this book is not merely wishful thinking but a realistic interpretation of what needs to be done to achieve perfection. Following the typical format of a lesson, the chapters are user friendly and brimming with adaptable ideas. The text is easily accessible and can be either followed directly or used to harvest ideas for upcoming lesson observations. As well as interesting tips for classroom tasks, Didau also offers a range of strategies to encourage deep thinking as well as demonstrating how excellent assessment for learning can lead to perfect English lessons every time.

Lisa-Jane Ashes, (AST) Author and
Creator of Reflections of a Learning Geek

If you can't learn from this book, it's probably because you're just four levels above Outstanding.

Kristian Still, Assistant Vice Principal,
Hamble Community Sports College

No one ever told me that being a teacher would be easy. No one ever told me that being a teacher of English would be even harder though. Language is a complex thing – the English language all the more so – and in our constant pursuit of academic excellence in the classroom there are times when we fall short.

Reading David Didau's book, after being a loyal follower of his unmissable Learning Spy blog, I clenched my fist in victorious appreciation on several occasions when that light bulb of possibility flashed above me. Mr Didau breaks down the English Lesson into four perfect parts – it is called `The Perfect English Lesson` after all – and with it, clarifies the true nature of what we should be doing in the English classroom.

Despite being in the classroom for 13 years, I found myself scribbling down an idea on almost every page. David's short book describes the creative and challenging ways we should be engaging our students and advancing their knowledge and skills in English. It glows with enthusiasm and bounds with energy; but, most importantly, it is crammed with wonderful ideas and useable tips which will change your practice tomorrow.

It did for me. Yesterday, I changed my approach to starter activities and had visual learning journeys on the board as students came in. Increased focus and engagement from the word go. David walks the reader through the practical importance of Carol Dweck, Dylan Wiliam and a host of other educational big hitters but it his own creative approach, coupled with an insistence on high expectations and even higher standards in the learners in his classroom, which shines through in every sentence.

There are not many books like this around and, while being a small book, fills a very large hole admirably. More importantly it is a book which makes me want to be better.

For the newly qualified English teacher, this book is perfect. For the experienced English teacher, it is no less so. There's a wealth of experience within these pages, but also love, joy, and compassion from a classroom practitioner on whom we should all model ourselves. Perhaps if we follow his advice we may find ourselves falling short just a little less often.

Kenny Pieper, English teacher in
a Scottish Secondary School

In an age when there's a tendency to clutch after ready-made gimmicks for every lesson, there's something hugely invigorating about David Didau's book. He reminds us that great English lessons are about relationships as well as content, but that they need to demonstrate our students' progress. He provides a range of ideas and approaches which can be customised to our own personalities and style to help us to teach lessons that aren't just outstanding against some Ofsted tick list, but genuinely outstanding. Recommended.

Geoff Barton, Headteacher, King Edward VI School

David's book arrives at a particularly opportune time. Changes in Ofsted criteria mean that we all have to up our game and focus on what really works in the classroom to promote outstanding progress. After 15 years of teaching and a lot of self-reflecting along the way, I have been looking to other professionals with bright ideas. I have found exactly that in David's book! His book is a treasure trove of teaching nuggets that make sense. He shares some sound teaching principles and some simply brilliant ideas. I have already implemented many changes in my lessons. I particularly like the way he integrates SOLO into his lesson planning and delivery, and the way the taxonomy is shared with and used by students. And it works! Another gem is the idea of learning journeys to spice up old boring LOs!

I will keep dipping in and out and being thankful for this inspirational book. A strongly recommended book for entrants to the profession and seasoned teachers alike!

Thanks for sharing, David.

Helene Galdin-O'Shea, English teacher,
Media Studies Curriculum Leader

THE PERFECT ENGLISH LESSON

ofsted

David Didau Edited by Jackie Beere

Independent Thinking Press

First published by

Independent Thinking Press
Crown Buildings, Bancyfelin, Carmarthen, Wales, SA33 5ND, UK
www.independentthinkingpress.com

Independent Thinking Press is an imprint of Crown House Publishing Ltd.

First published 2012. Reprinted 2012.

British Library Cataloguing-in-Publication Data
A catalogue entry for this book is available
from the British Library.

Print ISBN 978-1-78135-052-2
Mobi ISBN 978-1-78135-069-0
ePub ISBN 978-1-78135-070-6

Printed and bound in the UK by
Gomer Press, Llandysul, Ceredigion

For Olivia and Maddie

Contents

Acknowledgements

Since 2008 I've had the privilege of leading an outstanding team of English teachers at Priory Community School. Many of the ideas in this book have come about through working with such a passionate, enthusiastic, creative and, most of all, well-organised bunch of people. Other inspiration has come from some of the marvellous folks I've met on Twitter. Of these, special thanks must go to Jackie Beere for giving me the opportunity to write this book, Lisa Jane Ashes and Phil Beadle for allowing me to plagiarise some of their best stuff and Caroline Lenton and all at Independent Thinking Press for being so supportive.

A wise old bird once told me that all good teachers are thieves. I will admit to shamelessly snaffling any ideas I come across if they look interesting. That said, while I've tried to give credit where it's due I'm sure that there will be someone somewhere I've failed to properly acknowledge. Sorry.

Over my career I've had the opportunity to work with some incredible English teachers, but the one who's had to put up with the most is Rosie. My thanks.

Foreword

My first choice of career was journalism, writing first for a newspaper then for a computer magazine in London until a restless dissatisfaction with the commercial world took me into the classroom. I started teaching English in a secondary school in 1978. I had no English degree, a primary teaching qualification and had never taught English before. I was led to a cupboard full of books and told to pick one I might like to teach for the next few months. There were no schemes of work; no lesson plans, data, differentiation, engaging starters, collaborative activities or plenaries to measure progress. I made it up as I went along – and absolutely loved it!

Teaching English has always been characterised by opportunities to be creative and, quite rightly, enjoys high status amongst students and parents. It really is one of the most important subjects you do at school. In recent years that status has been ratcheted up several notches so that teaching English is as high status as it gets in secondary education. Along with that there is now extreme accountability at every Key Stage. Are your pupils making enough progress? Are they developing their literacy skills and using them across the curriculum? Are enough students getting level 4 in Year 6 or GCSE English grade C?

The sharp focus on the core subjects as a measure of school performance has made good English teachers highly valued and sought after – but has the learning experience for kids improved since those dim and distant days before the National Curriculum? A recent Ofsted research document 'Moving English Forward' suggests some English teachers slavishly follow lesson plans and a tick list strategy in their attempt to meet the examination (and inspection) criteria. But an outstanding English lesson is an opportunity to empower your learners, to awaken their interests and instil in them a love of reading. What David does in this book is capture some of the very best ways you can demonstrate those demanding outstanding Ofsted criteria in every lesson. The format he uses ensures that every question asked of an English teacher's performance can be answered to the highest possible standard – all with a sense of flair and fun!

David is perfectly placed to present these ideas to you as an experienced teacher and Head of English. With an enviable passion for the subject, he is also an avid blogger and tweeter, who shares and grows his ideas about teaching and learning. The ideas in this book are tried and tested so that they can be applied to your own context with confidence. Many of them are relevant to all subjects and across all phases of education.

My teaching of English evolved over the years through trial and error into the kind of responsive, engaging teaching that

David delivers every day and promotes in this book. Luckily for me I had time and space to grow – and make mistakes. English teachers today don't have that kind of luxury and so we need this book. Use it to guide you towards the essentials of the outstanding English lesson. Use it to add more strategies to your teaching repertoire. And tweak it to suit your context and your learners. This book can help your learners love our wonderful language and learn to use it with elegance and style to become powerful communicators.

Above all, use this book to make your English lessons outstanding and fun for your students – and for you too.

Jackie Beere
Tiffield, 2012

Introduction

Is there such a thing as
the perfect English lesson?

I passionately believe that by understanding a few simple principles and working hard to follow them, you can deliver the perfect English lesson. The very best English lessons provide engagement, motivation and genuine progress in the crucial skills of communication. I aim to lay out before you a smorgasbord of proven and successful titbits which you can mix together and use as and where you see fit.

If you're reading this book looking for tips to slot into a looming lesson observation you'll find plenty. But beware: there are no magic bullets that can turn you into an amazing teacher overnight. The perfect English lesson is not a matter of one-off charismatic delivery; it's about hard work and effort. It depends on thorough planning based on sound assessment for learning. And it's about consistently being there and having high expectations of, and a passionate belief in, the children in front of you.

Malcolm Gladwell and Matthew Syed have both written about the role of concerted and deliberate practice. Gladwell cites 10,000 hours of practice as the figure required for world-class mastery of your chosen field.[1] That doesn't mean you have to have been teaching for ten years before you're any good, but it does mean that by continually challenging yourself to be the best you can be you will always improve.

Like me, you probably think of yourself as a good teacher, capable of delivering an outstanding lesson given a following wind and a good night's sleep. Along the way you've also probably taught some shoddy lessons of which you were understandably ashamed. The temptation is to nail these failures into lead-lined coffins and never think of them again. But, although the process can be painful, they are worth dissecting and learning from. Samuel Beckett asked in one of my all time favourite educational exhortations, 'Ever tried? Ever failed? No matter. Try again. Fail again. Fail better.'[2]

The fact that you're reading this book shows that you want to learn to be an outstanding teacher. The good news is, if you care about it enough and work hard enough you *will* be outstanding – maybe not in every lesson but often enough to keep on trying. Assessment for learning guru Dylan Wiliam said we should 'ask teachers if they have anything to learn.

---

1. Malcolm Gladwell, *Outliers: The Story of Success* (Penguin, 2009); Matthew Syed, *Bounce: The Myth of Talent and the Power of Practice* (Fourth Estate, 2011).
2. Samuel Beckett, *Worstward Ho* (John Calder, 1983), p. 7.

If they say yes, work with them. If they say no, fire them.'[3] Remember: there is no failure, only feedback.

What makes English different?

Whilst all lessons share similarities, English lessons do contain some important differences. Unlike other subjects, English is not primarily about learning a body of core knowledge; it's much more about learning and practising skills.

We teach students mastery of their own tongue; we expose them to great cultural works; we give them time and space to articulate their nascent feelings. And we try to teach them about apostrophes. Where else, other than English lessons, are students at once creative and analytical? Where else are they exposed to such a breadth and variety of experiences?

As an English teacher you should strive to hone the hard-edged skill of analysis whilst simultaneously encouraging the fluff of creativity. There's some disagreement about whether you can actually teach creativity as a skill, but we can certainly expose young people to it and encourage them to use it – and we can absolutely give them knowledge of the 'rules' of whatever area we wish them to be creative in. Having a thorough grounding in these rules will give students the ability to know when to break them, which is one definition of creativity.

---

3. Dylan Wiliam, *Stopping people doing good things*, keynote address to the 18th National Conference of the Specialist Schools and Academies Trust, 21st Century Schooling/Excellence for All, Birmingham, UK, 23–26 November 2010.

This might seem over-simplistic, but the skill of writing is all about creativity whilst the skill of reading is firmly rooted in the ability to analyse. No one would suggest that reading and writing should be taught in isolation, and neither should creativity and analysis be seen as discrete entities.

Ofsted have commented that there is 'too little emphasis on creative and imaginative tasks'[4] in the teaching of writing. As English teachers we know this is something that we need value more highly. We know there's little joy in analysing poetry without having a stab at writing some. And it's dangerously negligent to get students to unpick the work of professional writers without then giving them the opportunity to use some of these tricks and techniques in writing of their own. This, of course, is the thinking behind the teaching sequence for writing: first you read it (analysis), then you write it (creativity).

The balance is easily lost. The pressure on schools to focus on exam skills means that 'Strategies that seek to engage students with the text [are] neglected in favour of approaches that [are] directly aimed at developing those skills needed for the type of analytical, literary-critical essay required in the GCSE examination.'[5] Our old friend Point Evidence Explain (PEE) is a particular offender, with students often being required to focus on a formulaic response that can remove any chance of truly connecting with a text.

---

4. Ofsted, *Moving English Forward: Action to Raise Standards in English* (15 March 2012). Ref: 110118. Available at http://www.ofsted.gov.uk/resources/moving-english-forward/, p. 25.
5. Ofsted, *Moving English Forward*, p. 16.

The perfect English lesson must strive to be a balance of these two components and to make them explicit. For every topic you intend to cover take time to consider this: where can you get students to analyse and how can you get them to be creative? Once you start thinking in this way, English teaching opens up a stunning vista of possibilities and your lessons will become more varied and challenging.

Myths about great teaching

The 2012 Ofsted report, *Moving English Forward*, identifies a number of 'myths' which many English teachers seem to mistakenly believe will impress inspectors. These include:

Myth 1: Lessons need to be fast paced

Actually faster is not better. While slow, ponderous lessons may result in students losing concentration, rattling through your lesson at breakneck pace is unlikely to result in much learning either. We should concentrate on the pace of the learning rather than the pace of the activities we've lovingly planned.

Myth 2: Lessons need to be packed with a range of activities

Not so. Many English teachers have been misled into believing that Ofsted want activities to last no longer than 10 minutes. Yes, this will keep students busy, but cramming activities into your lesson will not result in them learning more. In fact they're likely to learn less due to the lack of time available for consolidation. Instead lessons should have a clear focus on what it is that students need to learn and provide them with the opportunity to make progress in whatever this is. No one would expect a piece of controlled assessment to be shoehorned into 10 minute bursts; activities need 'to last only as long as is needed to ensure effective learning'.[6]

Myth 3: Lesson plans need to be massively detailed

Most schools insist on planning pro formas being completed for observed lessons. This is not in itself a bad thing, but if lessons are planned in excessive detail it's easy to lose sight of what it is students are meant to be learning. The advice from Ofsted is clear: plans should be simple, straightforward and concentrate on what you expect students to learn and how you'll make sure they've learnt it.

Myth 4: You should not deviate from your plan

Whilst the three- or four-part lesson structure may be a useful starting point, we need to have the confidence to change and adapt our plans if students' progress is better or worse than anticipated. An inspector will always be pleased to see teachers going off-piste if it means that students are given more opportunity to learn and make progress: 'The key con-

---

6. Ofsted, *Moving English Forward*, p. 13.

sideration should be the development of pupils' learning rather than sticking rigidly to a plan.'[7]

Myth 5: Learning needs to be reviewed every few minutes

There is a widespread belief that progress should be reviewed every 20 minutes come what may. But students need time if they are going to produce anything worthwhile. The temptation is to rush the 'actual work' so that we can get on with assessing progress. The belief that progress needs to be reviewed every few minutes is actually getting in the way of learning. We *know* this is wrong but often feel pressured to make it part of the 'Ofsted show'. Ofsted are very clear that this is unnecessary: 'significant periods of time were spent by teachers on getting pupils to articulate their learning, even where this limited their time to complete activities and thereby interrupted their learning!'[8]

In fact, what inspectors want to see are English lessons where students are given time to work independently for extended periods with teachers working less hard than their students. Ofsted criticise the fact 'that pupils rarely [have] extended periods to read, write or discuss issues in class'.[9] The perfect English lesson must devote time to developing these crucial skills.

---

7. Ofsted, *Moving English Forward*, p. 14.
8. Ofsted, *Moving English Forward*, p. 14.
9. Ofsted, *Moving English Forward*, p. 14.

One of the difficulties is that teachers feel they are being observed and therefore have to be seen doing something purposeful. The reality is that although the teacher is being judged, the inspector will be observing what the students are doing. As long as they're seen to be learning it really doesn't matter too much what you do.

Chapter 1
Planning the Perfect Lesson

Failing to plan is planning to fail. With a class of students preparing for a controlled assessment or an exam, your starting point should be to share the mark scheme and work out what it means. Just so with lesson observations. The following table shows Ofsted's generic criteria for outstanding lessons as well as the subject-specific guidance for English lessons.

Generic criteria (Ofsted framework)[1]	English-specific criteria (Ofsted guidance)[2]
Achievement of pupils	
■ Almost all pupils, including, where applicable, disabled pupils and those with special educational needs, are making rapid and sustained progress in most subjects over time given their starting points.	■ Pupils show high levels of achievement in the different areas of English (reading, writing, speaking and listening) and exhibit very positive attitudes towards the subject.
■ They learn exceptionally well and as a result acquire knowledge quickly and in depth and are developing their understanding rapidly in a wide range of different subjects across the curriculum, including those in the sixth form and areas of learning in the Early Years Foundation Stage.	■ They express their ideas fluently and imaginatively in both writing and speaking.
	■ They are very keen readers and show a mature understanding of a wide range of challenging texts, both traditional and contemporary.

1. Ofsted, *The Evaluation Schedule for the Inspection of Maintained Schools and Academies from January 2012* (30 March 2012). Ref. 090098. Available at http://www.ofsted.gov.uk/resources/evaluation-schedule-for-inspection-of-maintained-schools-and-academies-january-2012/.

These are our success criteria. Just like the students, if we know what they are and plan with them in mind then we are much more likely to teach a perfect English lesson.

But please bear in mind the following advice from Ofsted:

It is not unusual for inspectors to be presented with a three- or four-page lesson plan. A typical example might ask teachers to identify: learning aims and outcomes; resources; references to the National Curriculum and National Strategy objectives; links to a programme of learning skills; assessment opportunities; differentiation strategies, and so on. Lesson plans frequently expect teachers to refer to particular whole-school topics such as numeracy, information and communication technology or citizenship. Furthermore, the plan will include a detailed breakdown of the lesson, sometimes in five- or ten-minute chunks. It is not uncommon to find a lesson plan that includes (in addition to the features listed above) up to 500 words describing the lesson activities. This level of detail is counter-productive and does not necessarily lead to teaching that is clearly enough focused on specific learning outcomes for pupils. Previous English reports have commented that learning objectives were frequently over-ambitious for single lessons. Lesson plans should be simplified to encourage teachers to consider the central question: what is the key learning for pupils in this lesson and how can I bring it about?[3]

---

3. Ofsted, *Moving English Forward: Action to Raise Standards in English* (15 March 2012). Ref: 110118. Available at http://www.ofsted.gov.uk/resources/moving-english-forward/, p. 47.

Does the plan relate to the sequence of teaching?

An inspector will be looking to see what happened before your lesson and what's likely to happen next. This can be addressed very simply and straightforwardly by getting the students to use what they learnt last lesson at the beginning of this lesson. In a perfect English lesson you will already have acted on the formative assessment that concluded the previous lesson and produced tailored written feedback to individuals on where exactly any misconceptions lurk and how precisely to beat them into submission.

You need to consider how this lesson plan fits into the wider picture of skills and content that you ought to be covering. Have a look at the Learning Loop model (see page 37) as a way of building in repeated opportunities for students to master knowledge and skills.

You also need to have medium- and long-term plans which indicate the direction of your planning. At the end of the unit, students should know and be able to do a number of things. It is therefore essential to demonstrate that your planning is underpinned by Assessment Focuses and GCSE Assessment Objectives. In our perfect English lesson we need to show that students are learning something which develops skills and expands knowledge; something which they will have encountered before and which they will encounter again.

Does the planning demonstrate high expectations and challenge?

The most important single factor influencing learning is what the learner already knows. Ascertain this and teach him accordingly.

David Ausubel[4]

As with so much else, the success of your lesson is dependent on embedded assessment for learning. If you know what your students know, you can plan lessons that are pitched to challenge everyone.

Challenge is a tough balancing act. The work you plan should not be so difficult that the students can't do it, but it should be demanding. What makes the impossible merely difficult is providing clear routes through the thickets so that students can see how to do whatever it is you want them to do.

In an English lesson this is done by mapping the Assessment Focuses (AFs) for reading, writing and speaking and listening into your long-term planning to ensure that everything you do is developing these crucial skills. If we have a clear understanding of where our students are and what they need to learn to make progress, then we will be able to plan engaging and challenging lessons.

---

4. David Ausubel, *Educational Psychology: A Cognitive View* (Holt, Rinehart & Winston, 1968), p. vi; quoted in John Hattie, *Visible Learning: A Synthesis of Over 800 Meta-Analyses Relating to Achievement* (Routledge, 2009),

To enjoy doing something, we need to be pretty good at doing it. For instance, to enjoy reading we need to know 90–95% of the words in a text.[5]

In order to show that progress is being made we are expected to know everyone's 'target' grades/levels and to have shared this information with the students. Communicating this can raise several issues:

1. By giving students grades you start moving away from assessment for learning, even if you wrap up the grade in lots of formative comments. Slapping grades on students' work is often used in an attempt to improve results. But it doesn't work. Dylan Wiliam says: 'when students get marks and comments, they first look at their own mark and then at their neighbour's. They hardly ever read the comments.'[6]

2. The 'targets' we're sharing are nothing of the sort. They're estimates derived from statistical analysis and bear little or no relation to the students sitting in front of us.

3. It seems clear that formative assessment encourages growth mindsets, whereas grades (especially target grades) encourage students to have a fixed view of their intelligence and potential.

---

5. E. D. Hirsch Jr, *The Knowledge Deficit, Closing the Shocking Education Gap for American Children* (Houghton Mifflin, 2009), p.60.
6. Dylan Wiliam and Paul Black, *Feedback is the best nourishment* (TES 4 October 2002) http://www.tes.co.uk/article.aspx?storycode=369889.

But how would an inspector or school leader respond to being told that you didn't let students know their target grades?

If we must have students knowing their target grades then let's at least make them a force for good. My suggestion is to hassle your school's data manager to provide you with the statistical underpinning of the students' target grades and provide each student with something which looks like this:

G	F	E	D	C	B	A	A*
0.1%	0.1%	0.6%	6.6%	31.7%	39.2%	18.2%	3.5%

This shows the likelihood of the student achieving a particular GCSE result based on their achievement at Key Stage 2. It is much more motivating than just telling an individual that they're supposed to get a Level 5, a D grade or whatever it is they're 'predicted'.

Take the time and trouble to alert the observer to the fact that you have supplied all the students in the class with this information by saying something along the lines of, 'Now children, turn to the inside front cover of your thoroughly marked exercise books and refresh your memories of the chance you have of achieving a grade higher than your target grade' (in the case of the student above this is the dark grey box).

Students need to believe that the biggest difference between the people who achieved an A instead of a B is that they worked harder and wanted it more. Armed with this sort of information they should work their metaphorical socks off.

Is the plan appropriate for the learning needs of all groups of pupils?

This is a big one. It could be successfully argued that every child is vulnerable in their own special way and that we should cater for their needs appropriately. It's a good idea to put together a dossier on every student you teach in order to be able to wheel it out in the event of an observation. If you can show how all your students' 'special needs' have been catered for the inspector should be impressed. More importantly though, the act of collating this information will provide you with a full and detailed knowledge of your students and will, one would hope, enable you to plan for their learning needs.

Your able students will be encouraged to analyse and evaluate; dyslexic students might have access to phonic charts to help with spelling; less confident students need to be given safe opportunities to develop their ability to speak in front of audiences; and so on.

Stripped to its essentials what we are looking for here is *differentiation*. It might sound self-evident, but it seems reasonable to point out that differentiation is the process of acknowledging that every child is different and treating them accordingly. In terms of classroom application, the first thing that even a cursory study of the subject reveals is that there are various different ways one can go about differentiating. These include (1) assessment, (2) outcome, (3) support and (4) task.

1. **Differentiating by assessment** is arguably formative assessment by another name. This is a good thing. Various researchers have confirmed that formative assessment and feedback are the most beneficial activities any English teacher can be doing. Regular and thorough marking of students' work will mean that you are able to identify exactly what levels of differentiation your students require and ensure that you can praise their efforts in your care to help foster that all important growth mindset. Try marking work with questions that students must respond to:

   ■ How could you vary your punctuation for impact?

   ■ What is the most powerful word in your quotation?

   ■ How could you build on or challenge your partner's opinion?

2. **Differentiating by outcome** usually involves a combination of the 'All must ...', 'Most should ...' and 'Some could ...' learning objectives. However, this runs the risk of fixing your students' beliefs about their ability (or perceived lack thereof) and ensuring that they're too frightened to try anything that looks hard as that would mean they'd fail. Again. Differentiating in this way announces that you're prepared to accept the

minimum that 'all' the students are capable of. It is 'a definition of low expectations'.[7]

3. **Differentiating by support.** There's no way to meaningfully support every student in your class whether or not you're fortunate enough to have a classroom assistant in your lesson. The most effective way to use your classroom assistant is to team-teach with them whilst ensuring that students are arranged to support each other. If you don't have a teaching assistant, allowing students to assume the role of teacher can help them deepen their understanding of a subject. Even better, it provides a safe way for them to take risks without the fear of being ridiculed for 'getting it wrong' in front of the whole class. Best of all, it doesn't require much effort on a day-to-day basis. As long as you've worked out your seating plan to ensure that students are paired up for sound educational reasons, all will be well.

4. **Differentiating by task** is the one we all hate and feel so guilty about. Yes, your lessons will be better if you do it. Yes, your students will learn more effectively. But, my goodness, you'll suffer for it. In order to properly differentiate by task, teachers need to design several distinct lessons which students can access at different levels. This might involve producing a variety of resources appropriate for the varying levels of ability represented in your class, such as writing frames and

---

7. Phil Beadle, *How To Teach* (Crown House Publishing, 2010), p. 194.

other scaffolds. The only manageable way to approach this type of differentiation is to plan: well-thought out and properly differentiated questions can be really effective in ensuring that all students are suitably challenged. Effective, differentiated questioning should be part of your practice on a daily basis but the faff and hassle involved in creating endlessly varied worksheets should be reserved for special occasions.

Setting out the room to maximise learning

The key is what is going on in each student's mind – because influencing these minds is the point of the lesson.

John Hattie[8]

Teaching doesn't necessarily lead to learning; learning is a collaborative process and depends on dialogue. If desks are set out in rows, students are forced to face front and pay attention to the teacher. Whilst they can compare ideas with their desk partner, any kind of group discussion is made difficult.

If tables are arranged in groups then extended discourse, which is the basis of all great English lessons, becomes much more likely. This will allow our lessons to make use of the private world of students and the way they learn from each other. According to Graham Nuthall, 25% of everything students learn they learn from each other or from directing their

---

8. John Hattie, *Visible Learning for Teachers* (Routledge, 2012), p. 33.

own learning.[9] The perfect English lesson should allow for paired discussions and collaborative group work as well as an opportunity for students to work on their own.

In an ideal world we would infinitely vary our groupings. The truth is that moving desks about is a drag (literally) and you won't have time to do it several times a day, let alone several times a lesson. The solution is to organise your desks into five groups of six (with a couple of spares for especially large classes) which will make it easy to move from one activity to the next without lugging desks about. Ideally, you will also leave space in the centre of the room for presentations and drama activities.

Is there a 'safe' learning environment?

A positive, caring, respectful climate in the classroom is a prior condition to learning.

John Hattie[10]

At the most basic level there should be an atmosphere in your lesson where everyone feels OK to take risks and get stuff wrong without being subjected to mocking catcalls or ritual humiliation. Obviously no one's going to learn if they don't feel safe and we must make sure we're fair and predictable in our interactions, particularly when students ask us for help.

9. Graham Nuthall, *The Hidden Lives of Learners* (NZCER Press, 2007), p.156.
10. Hattie, *Visible Learning for Teachers*, p. 70.

A positive learning environment is one in which it's safe to learn. Perhaps if we approached our classes with a 100% positive attitude the mindset of our students would change and the classroom would become a safe place to learn – a place where all students make three (and perhaps four) levels of progress. Even *those* kids!

Beware of cultivating what Carol Dweck calls a 'fixed mind-set'[11] as it can lead to students struggling with failure. They will develop a fixed view of intelligence or ability in a particular area: they're either good at something or they're not. Often people with fixed mindsets want to achieve without making effort; if something is hard that means they're not good enough. Success should be effortless. If they fail, there must be an excuse: it must be someone else's fault. Admitting that the fault might be theirs is too uncomfortable. Needless to say, this is not a great mindset for learning. On the other hand, growth mindset bods enjoy learning and making an effort for their own sakes. They are intrinsically motivated to try, fail and try again.

We've all encountered students who fit into these two categories, and possibly we have a 'fixed' view of them. The good news is that we can all cultivate a growth mindset. Students (and teachers) can be taught to see failure as progress and to be intrinsically motivated to learn. Dweck asserts that anyone is capable of succeeding. Instead of asking 'How can I teach these kids?', ask 'How can I teach them?' This is the

---

11. Dweck, C., *Mindset* (Ballantine, 2006).

preferred mindset for a teacher wishing to deliver the perfect English lesson.

So how can we teach students to have a growth mindset?

1. Teach students to adopt a growth mindset that views learning as a journey and effort as the path to mastery.

2. Praise effort, not ability. When we say, 'You're really good at writing', we are fixing their view of how intelligent they are. Saying, 'You really worked hard on using a range of sentence starts' reinforces the fact that the effort we make is the biggest factor in our likely success. It also shows that you value the *process* of learning over the end product.

3. Use formative assessment to help students understand exactly what they need to do to be successful. Avoid giving grades wherever possible – these just fix mindsets and make students either give up because they think they're crap, or coast because they think they're clever.

4. Have very high standards: don't accept minimal effort and insist that students produce work that they can take pride in. Don't accept excuses and don't make any excuses for them. Insist that all work is proofread before it's handed in. Warn students that they will be copying out their work if they fail to do this.

5. Don't offer extrinsic rewards – they prevent students from valuing the learning and remove intrinsic motivation.[12]

6. Build a nurturing environment where it is safe to make mistakes. Failure must be welcomed with open arms; and students must be shown that we learn by making mistakes. There's nothing like mastering something you thought you couldn't do to give the old self-confidence a boost.

7. Above all, don't give up on the difficult ones; that's what they're expecting so prove them wrong. *Know* that they can achieve.

---

12. Giving out sweets or offering a film viewing in exchange for good behaviour or effort actually undermines students' ability to learn for its own sake. You may even want to think carefully about whether reward points or praise letters are actually productive.

Chapter 2
The Start of the Lesson

You never get a second chance to make a first impression. The perfect English starter is all about setting the tone, both for your students and for the inspector. Make sure you have a plan to give them and somewhere for them to sit. Whenever I have a visitor to my classroom I have a student primed, ready to jump up and welcome them in and explain whatever it is they're learning. This way you can focus on the lesson and the inspector can probe the students about whether or not you're any cop.

Does the lesson get off to a flying start?

This is all about students learning as soon as they enter the classroom, which is sometimes called 'bell work'. The outstanding lesson will have an activity ready to go the moment the first students arrive. They should be able to get on with it without having to wait for stragglers to turn up, and it should be something interesting and engaging that will make them want to find out more. A shock and awe approach works well here – anything unfamiliar, interactive and designed to make students think will fit the bill. Use dramatic music, surprising images, film played at the wrong speed; ask them relevant and thought provoking questions; give them puzzles to solve; dress up in costume; get them moving, doing and asking questions about the learning that is to come.

A careful scrutiny of the research[1] shows that the first 10 minutes of the lesson can have a massive impact on learning and progress. To spend this time most effectively use one or more or, ideally, all three of the following strategies:

1. Show a visual representation of the learning that will take place during the lesson.

2. Set learning intentions that are not outcome based but focused on what will be learned.

3. Use questioning to recall prior learning.

---

1. Geoff (no relation to 1980s rocker Tom) Petty shows that using this strategy along with a traditional learning objective, plus an activity which links to students' prior learning, has an effect size of 2.66. This is a little technical for anyone who hasn't yet encountered Professor John Hattie's research into effect sizes. The basic principle is this: Hattie calls an effect size of at least 0.4 as the 'hinge point' at which point a strategy can be described as 'effective'. An effect size of 'only' 1.0 is typically associated with:
    *   Advancing learners' achievement by one year, or improving the rate of learning by 50%.
    *   A two-grade leap in GCSE, e.g. from a C to an A grade.
    An effect size of 1.0 is enormous. An effect size of 2.66 is the mother lode! I'm not sure I want to attempt calculating the impact this amounts to in terms of potential GCSE results: it's enough to know that it's clearly worth trying. See Geoff Petty, *Evidence-Based Teaching: A Practical Approach*, 2nd edn (Nelson Thornes, 2009) and John Hattie, *Visible Learning: A Synthesis of Over 800 Meta-Analyses Relating to Achievement* (Routledge, 2009).

No surprises here then: the second two strategies in particular are things we've surely all been doing for ages. The trick is to combine all three.

So how do we go about the visual representation of the learning? The idea itself is incredibly simple: at the beginning of the lesson, draw a picture or provide images which relate to the learning which will take place during the lesson. That's it. A visual learning objective.

I recommend you prepare these in advance; call them Learning Journeys and display on a slide as the learners come into the lesson. Here's a couple of examples from a lesson on the theme of Steinbeck's *Of Mice and Men*.

A Learning Journey slide can seem a little confusing at first, but students will soon start puzzling over and discussing what the lesson will be about.

Here's what some of my students said about the slides:

'I like it because it makes you think more about what the lesson will be about.'

'When I see the Learning Journey on the board I start trying to work it out. I think it's a good way to start the lesson.'

'At first I hated it because it was more effort than copying down the objective but now I think it helps get me more involved in what we're doing.'

Make sure you show the Learning Journey slide a few times during the lesson. This is a great way into reviewing progress and assessing where we are and where we need to go.

You could ask students to write their own learning objectives based on what they think they will be doing in the lesson.

Is there a recap of previous learning?

Learning is a liminal process, at the boundary between control and chaos.

Dylan Wiliam[2]

---

2. Dylan Wiliam, 'Assessment, Learning and Technology: Prospects at the Periphery of Control', keynote address to the 14th International Conference of the Association for Learning Technology, ALT-C 2007: Beyond Control, Nottingham, UK, 4–6 September 2007.

Learning is about making connections between the background knowledge, experiences, interests and motivations which students bring *to* the classroom with what they encounter *in* the classroom.

Because of their diversity of experience, roughly one third of what students learn will be unique to them.[3] Let me put that another way: one in three things a student will have learned by the end of a teaching sequence will not be known by any other student! In a class of 30 students that's a lot of unique knowledge.

You may have a clear learning objective which you intend all students to learn but there is much that can easily get in the way of our efforts to direct learning. The main reason for students not learning is that they lack sufficient prior knowledge to integrate new information into their existing mental maps, and their poor over-burdened brains simply raise the white flag and bugle their surrender.

Knowledge is not tiny bits that we can count and represent by numbers, but a network of logically interconnected ideas, beliefs and generalisations structured so it can be searched and used to work out and evaluate new ideas.

Graham Nuthall[4]

Learning is more likely to take place if your lessons are memorable. Students don't just learn the English curriculum we trot out before them; they also remember the context in

---

3. Graham Nuthall, *The Hidden Lives of Learners* (NZCER Press, 2007), p. 50.
4. Graham Nuthall, *The Hidden Lives of Learners* (NZCER Press, 2007), p. 154.

which they learnt it. If something dramatic and exciting happens then they'll retain a vivid memory of it and use it as an anchor for the concept it was used to teach.

How students experience an activity is as much a part of what they learn as the intended curriculum content. If they listen to a lecture or complete a worksheet they are learning to be passive and to fill in gaps in someone else's work. If they are active in their learning then they'll find out that learning happens when you take responsibility and manage yourself.

Making sure that every lesson recaps what has gone before is a simple and efficient way of helping to ensure that students remember the stuff we're trying to teach them.

Points to keep in mind

■ 'Thinking' cannot happen independently – it has to be tied to what students already know. Therefore we have to design lessons that use their existing knowledge and understanding. For example, students need to know about the parts of speech before they can construct and deconstruct sentences.

■ We have to build in opportunities for students to revisit new ideas. I don't mean that we should simply repeat lessons; the information should be presented in different ways which allows them to see connections with what has gone before.

■ In order to monitor what students are learning we need to assess what they know at the beginning of a teaching sequence or scheme of learning and compare this to what they know at the end. We've already observed that everyone will start off knowing different things and this will result in them learning different things.

■ Be selective. If we're going to use every strategy outlined above in every lesson then we're probably not going to be able to get through everything in the curriculum. We need to decide which is more important: teaching or learning. Do we want to make sure that we teach as much as possible, or that students learn as much as possible? You can't have both. We should therefore focus on those areas which provide the biggest payoffs for students. Sadly, as English teachers, this means we can't always cover the range of texts in the depth we'd like; instead we need to concentrate on extracts that provide opportunities to link to other parts of the course.

■ Because much of what students learn comes from their own and their peers' experience we need to be aware of the culture outside the classroom. We will benefit from knowing what they're interested in, what they're good at and who is popular. If we allow opportunities for different students to shine at different times then we make sure that all the children we teach have a chance to excel – not just the 'bright' ones. Setting up tasks which require a combination of skills and knowledge is perhaps the best way of ensuring that there is the prospect for everyone to learn because everyone will get to connect new information to different sets of prior knowledge. For example, you could begin the study of *Romeo and Juliet* by getting students to share and explore their own experiences of relationships and family conflict.

■ Because students learn best when self-selecting and self-generating experiences we need to teach them how to do this better. We need to deliver curriculum content in such a way that they will also be taught effective ways of learning it. Over time we can train them in the good habits which they can apply on their own to learn new concepts. So if we want students to be better at reading comprehension, we need a relentless attention on extending vocabulary and learning interesting facts about the world beyond where they live. We need to expose them to the 'canon' and give them the skills and curiosity to persevere in the face of difficult or unfamiliar language.

Sharing the big picture and looping the learning[5]

It has become received wisdom that students will only be motivated to learn if they understand why they are doing whatever it is we want them to do. Sharing the big picture allows them to connect the dots. Instead of having to start

---

5. Learning Loops seem to be a product of the zeitgeist as much as anything else, but I can attest to the fact that Hannah Thomas, an advanced skills teacher at Priory Community School, arrived at the concept and the name entirely independently.

The Learning Loop model

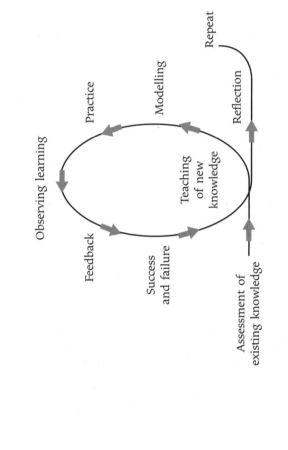

Source: David Didau with Hannah Thomas

from scratch every time we want students to analyse a writer's use of language, it's worth reminding them of the last time they used this skill. Within the context of GCSE English, students will have to use their language analysis skills in various pieces of controlled assessment in the English Language exam and in both English Literature exams. If we make it clear often enough that this is the same stuff we do in lessons, we can hope that eventually it will seep into their brains at some unconscious level.

Looping learning (see page 37) is a way of getting students to repeat and therefore learn complex skill sets without them becoming demotivated by tedious rote exercises. If our lessons contain learning loops which provide students with plenty of opportunities for the practice of new skills and varied ways to apply new concepts, then we can be sure that learning will start to leak through into long-term memory. In English this should be fairly straightforward: take, for instance, the skills needed to do well at reading. We need to make explicit the fact that whether they're reading poetry, a newspaper article, a Shakespeare play or a text message, they're using the same set of skills: retrieval, understanding, interpretation and analysis. Each time we teach a 'new' topic we should make sure that students understand that they need to do what they did last time.

The Learning Loop model can be tailored to fit any part of the curriculum. For example, to help students learn how to write in a way which meets the needs of different audiences and purposes we can design a series of learning loops to accomplish this. If this cycle is repeated at least three times then students will be well on the way to having learnt a fairly complex skill. Because this knowledge stands a good chance of being embedded into long-term memory, when they are required to write for new audiences and purposes it should be easily retrievable. This should mean that you get less of those, 'Sir, I don't know what to do' moments.

Are learning objectives clear and appropriate in number?

We know that students can't take responsibility for their own learning if they don't know what they are expected to learn. Students produce better work if they know and understand the learning objective, which is why learning objectives should be shared with pupils in advance and displayed visually during lessons.

I'm going to go out on a limb here and suggest that, at least as far as learning objectives are concerned, more is not merrier. We need to be absolutely clear exactly what it is that we want students to know/understand or be able to do by the end of the lesson. More than that, we want them to be able to show some (if not exemplary) progress. Multiple objectives only muddle up students and slow down your finely crafted lesson. I'd suggest one clear subject-specific objective. The most important thing for you, the teacher, is to be crystal clear about what it is the students are supposed to be learning and to have a coherent plan for how students will produce evidence which shows progress against this objective.

But what about the differentiated objective? Isn't this more than one objective? A well-differentiated objective can be accessible on several different levels without much work on anyone's part. All it requires is teaching students the meaning of a number of key verbs. Consider for instance the following objective:

To understand how to explain the effects of presentational devices.

What's the key word here? What happens if we substitute 'explain' with 'explore' or 'analyse' or 'evaluate'? The objective of the lesson remains essentially the same but we can now ask students to choose the point at which they will access it, so that the objective could become:

To understand how to analyse the effects of presentational devices.

It doesn't take a genius to see how these verbs can be related to the GCSE mark scheme. Obviously this will only work if you've put some effort into teaching students the difference between these different skills beforehand. The words 'explain', 'explore', 'analyse' and 'evaluate' must be referred to regularly.

While we're on the subject, it's worth noting that as far as Ofsted are concerned, learning objectives are the same as learning intentions and are probably not too dissimilar from aims or outcomes.

Are learning objectives shared?

Sharing objectives with students has now become so ingrained that I can't remember the last time I went into a classroom where the objective was not displayed. Make no mistake though: simply writing your objective on the board is not enough.

Our objectives should be shared with students in as creative and interesting a way as possible. Don't just get students to copy them down in their books and tick them at the end of the lesson. What follows are a few ideas for interesting ways to introduce learning objectives into your lessons.[6]

Missing key word

This is every bit as simple as it looks – simply leave out a word from the objective and ask the class to decide what they think it is. It's an absolute doddle to do; in fact slightly less work than normal as you actually write one less word!

To be able to use different ways to start _ _ _ _ _ _ _ _ _ _ .

Minimal effort is required and the students will be thinking about and interacting with the objective in a different way. (No prizes for guessing the missing key word was 'sentences'.)

---

6. Many of these suggestions have been collated by Kristian Still: http://www.kristianstill.co.uk/wordpress/2011/10/19/51-ways-to-introduce-learning-objectives/.

Anagram

Why not jumble up your learning objective as an anagram? Mixing up the whole thing might be a bit mad and potentially take forever, so just jumble the key words. If we take an objective like 'To be able to use reading strategies to discuss a text' we only need to make anagrams out of 'reading' and 'strategies' to end up with something wonderful like:

To be able to use a greased tie string to discuss a text.[7]

If the objective links in some way to work they've recently been doing (and it should – see page 32) then it won't take the students long to work out the answer. It will, however, focus them on the key words and just maybe they'll think about the objective in a way they wouldn't normally.

Facebook status

Mr Didau

wants you to be able to proofread & redraft your work

Like – Comment – 2 minutes ago

---

7. My favourite online anagram maker is Angelfire: http://www.angelfire.com/biz/WLAW/anagram.html/.

Students really enjoy the gimmick of the learning objective looking like a Facebook status update. Also, they all heartily enjoy giving it a thumbs down to signify their opprobrium. So far, so silly. But making them comment on the status is where it gets interesting. Getting them to write their own status updates is also a neat way to round off a lesson.

Expand a sentence

This is basically getting the students to add 'because' to the end of the objective and adding their reasons why it might be worth doing. For instance, if your objective is that students are able to proofread and redraft their work, the expanding sentence could be, 'Proofreading and redrafting will improve your writing because ...' This is dead easy to do and gets them effortlessly thinking about the learning they're about to do.

Order the learning

The basic premise of this one is to take the words of the objective and arrange them in order of importance. So, in a lesson on the ending of *Of Mice and Men* you might want students to consider the techniques Steinbeck uses and to explore their reactions.

Learning objective:

■ To be able to evaluate the impact of the techniques Steinbeck uses in section 5 of the novel.

■ Rearrange the words in the objective in order of importance (as a hierarchy).

This provokes lots of discussion and the hierarchical nature of the task lends itself to the novel as you will have been doing lots of thinking on power and where the different characters fit into the ranch's hierarchy.

One thing to make clear is not to bother with words like 'the' and 'of', but aside from that, what *is* the most important word? Who cares? The students are thinking and that's all that matters.

Connected words

Give groups different key words from the objective to focus on and ask them to come up with as many connected words as possible in 1 minute. The key words from the objective 'To be able to explore the ways power is presented in *Of Mice and Men*' might be 'explore', 'ways', 'power' and 'presented'. Students often come up with some amazing ideas which can spark some really interesting discussion. In one lesson a group of students made a connection between 'explore' and 'look around'. This provoked an extended debate on what 'looking around' might look like in their controlled assessments. It's ridiculously easy to do and makes for a decidedly purposeful start to the lesson.

Multiple choice

Hinge questions are a jolly useful way of assessing students' progress, but they're also a good way to introduce your learning objective. The idea is to provide a list of statements and then get students to work out what the actual objective is. If the objective was 'To be able to proofread and redraft your work', you would ask the class which of the following statements they think would make the most impact on the quality of their work:

- You should make your work as neat as possible.
- You should count the exact number of words you have written.
- You should read through your work and check you have met all the success criteria.
- You should use the time at the end of an exam to do a bit more writing.

This is useful for exploding misconceptions as well as getting the students themselves to justify the use of success criteria. Hearing comments like, 'If you don't use the success criteria how can you know how well you've done?' is music to my ears. It's a bit of trouble to think of the statements, but the impact is potentially tremendous.

3-2-1

The idea with this is to get the students thinking about what they do and don't know about a topic as well as encouraging them to think creatively. They start by listing what they know and then asking questions about what they might need to know, before finishing with a striking and unique comparison.

3 things I know about the topic are ...

2 questions I have about the topic are ...

1 analogy: 'The topic is like ... because ...'

If the objective is 'To be able to vary the way sentences start', students need to work through the three steps and will hopefully write something along these lines:

3 things I know about sentences are that they have full stops at the end, they start with a capital letter and they have to have a verb in them.

2 questions I have about sentences are how do you use commas and what is a subordinate clause.

1 analogy: 'Sentences are like roads because the reader has to be able to travel down them to get where they're going.'

This requires a little thinking about but once you're clear on what to do it's very simple. You will probably have to model a few analogies to ensure they know what is expected as this is certainly the stage they manage least well. But that's fine:

the students are thinking and engaged. What more could one ask from a learning objective?

SOLO objective

As well as it's many other miraculous properties, the SOLO Taxonomy (Structure of Observed Learning Outcomes) developed by John Biggs,[8] is also handy for introducing objectives and many teachers have seen the difference it can make to students' understanding.

It starts with an idea (the uni-structural level) and then develops into lots of ideas (the multi-structural level). We then start to see the relationship between these ideas (the relational level) before finally being able to have abstract, conceptual ideas (extended abstract level).

It's fairly straightforward to get to multi-structural; students just have to know stuff. This is where many students get bogged down and simply churn out more and more things they know. In our rush to move them on, we must not neglect this vitally important stage; without a secure knowledge base students will be unable to make meaningful connections and will fail to see the relationship between the things they know. As soon as they can see that making progress requires something beyond simply spilling out more knowledge, they're able to take the plunge from shallow to deep understanding.

---

8. Biggs, John and Collis, Kelvin, *Evaluating the Quality of Learning: The SOLO Taxonomy* (Academic Press, 1982).

The SOLO levels make it easy for students to see how well they're working and what they need in order to make progress, but it's also worth having a look at the following table to see what is exemplified for each level.

SOLO level	Verbs
Uni-structural	define, identify, name, draw, find, label, match, follow a simple procedure
Multi-stuctural	describe, list, outline, complete, continue, combine
Relational	sequence, classify, compare & contrast, explain (cause & effect), analyse, form an analogy, organise, distinguish, question, relate, apply
Extended abstract	generalise, predict, evaluate, reflect, hypothesise, theorise, create, prove, justify, argue, compose, prioritise, design, construct, perform

In a lesson on the powerful forces at work in *Of Mice and Men* you might get students to decide where their level of understanding lies at the start of the lesson:

■ I don't know anything about powerful forces in section 1 of *Of Mice and Men* (pre-structural).

- I know one thing about powerful forces in section 1 of *Of Mice and Men* (uni-structural).

- I know a few things about powerful forces in section 1 of *Of Mice and Men* (multi-structural).

- I can use the things I know about powerful forces to explain their impact on the story and characters in section 1 of *Of Mice and Men* (relational).

- I can use what I know about powerful forces in section 1 of *Of Mice and Men* to be able to speculate about how they will impact on the rest of the novel (extended abstract).

The clever bit is to ask students to come up with an objective which might help them move to at least the relational if not the extended abstract level. SOLO is marvellous for getting students to see how to make progress. It takes a fair bit of time to get your head around the four levels of understanding but once they're secure, you (and your students) will be able to move through them with the grace of a young gazelle (see the Appendix).

Learning continuum[9]

The idea is that the learning objective for a lesson should not be viewed as something static. Students can achieve outcomes that meet the objective at different levels. Isn't this just differentiated outcomes? Well, yes, but the difference

---

9. The idea for learning continuums comes from Jackie Beere's *The Perfect Ofsted Lesson* (Crown House Publishing, 2010).

here is that the emphasis is placed on students continuing on through the learning journey over the course of the lesson.

If your objective is to develop your ability to diversify the assessment for learning techniques you have in your armoury, then the three outcome boxes on page 51 provide a useful checklist to monitor your progress in meeting the objective. The objective is written within an arrow to represent a clear sense of progress and direction: this knowledge is going somewhere; this skill can be developed to different levels of expertise.

The first box could be viewed as a baseline or starting point; the all/everyone part of a differentiated outcome or the first checkpoint at which learning is reviewed. The outcome boxes should be used as review checkpoints to show students the progress they have made so far, with the expectation being that they should try to reach the third box by the end of the lesson.

Example 1

The first example is a continuum used with a mixed ability Year 9 GCSE class. The outcomes are linked to GCSE grades so students can relate their success against performance criteria with which they are familiar:[10]

---

10. ToPTiP is a simple mnemonic to help students remember when to start a new paragraph (Topic, Person, Time and Place).

Example 1

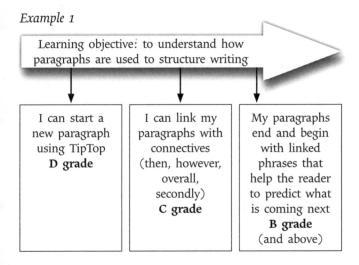

Learning objective: to understand how paragraphs are used to structure writing

| I can start a new paragraph using TipTop **D grade** | I can link my paragraphs with connectives (then, however, overall, secondly) **C grade** | My paragraphs end and begin with linked phrases that help the reader to predict what is coming next **B grade** (and above) |

Example 2

Learning objective: to be able to work out meaning using clues and interpret language

| I can EXPLAIN what words reveal about the poem's meaning **C grade** | I can EXPLORE words and ideas to see alternative meanings of the poem **B grade** | I can ANALYSE and EVALUATE words and ideas to work out the writer's intentions and impact on the reader **A - A*** |

Example 2

This goes further and links these grades to the language of Bloom's (or SOLO) taxonomy. This helps students to consider the thinking skills required to progress on their learning journeys.

This is a fantastic tool for getting students to think about their progress and the direction of their learning. It's easy to stop the lesson at any point and ask students to mark an X to show how far they've travelled, or even to ask them to get up and physically position themselves against an arrow on the classroom wall.

Leave it until the end[11]

There are times when you just don't want to tell students what the objective is at the beginning of the lesson. Maybe it will spoil a surprise or perhaps you think the students' learning will in some way be limited. Whatever the reason, as long as you do actually have an objective there shouldn't be a problem.

Here's an example of a lesson on *An Inspector Calls* in which the students had to guess the objective. I made the possibly spurious decision to use hula hoops and wanted them to think about how Priestley makes us reflect on guilt and responsibility. This was my plan:

---

11. This was inspired by Phil Beadle's *Dancing about Architecture: A Little Book of Creativity* (Crown House Publishing, 2011).

Chapter 2

■ Inform students that today's lesson would take place outside and that they would need their copy of the play and a hula hoop.

■ Give out the hula hoops and hope that at least one student is sufficiently talented to give a short tutorial.

■ Pose question: 'What do hula hoops and Act 3 of *An Inspector Calls* have in common?'

■ Explain the task. Students to work in teams of five or six; they are to read Act 3 whilst simultaneously hula hooping. If the hula hoop is not 'in motion' then the team has to go back to the beginning of the page they're at and start again. Differentiation: the less able are allowed to use their arm to keep the hula hoop spinning.

■ Check learning.

■ Students to suggest possible objectives for the lesson and state whether they have met them.

After 20 minutes of struggling to read, it was firmly established that it is pretty much impossible to have a successful group reading of a play whilst hula hooping. But did we learn anything else?

My favourite conversation in response to the hula hoop/guilt debate went like this:

Student 1: *I learnt that you feel guilty when you drop the hula hoop because your team has to start the page over again.*

Student 2: *I didn't feel guilty when I dropped it.*

Student 3: *That's because you're Mrs Birling! (For those who don't know, Sybil Birling is a character who refuses to take responsibility for her actions.)*

Other interesting outcomes included the observation that the structure of the play is like hula hooping because it just goes round in circles with nothing really changing. Awesome! It might have taken me hours to have 'taught' that idea.

Some of the learning objectives the students came up with at the end of the lesson included:

- To be able to work as a team and accept responsibility for failing your team.
- To discover how Priestly uses the theme of guilt and responsibility in *An Inspector Calls*.
- To be able to concentrate on a task and cooperate effectively.
- To be able to cope with failure.

All of these are laudable objectives. But had I chosen just one of them, how much would I have limited the opportunities for learning?

To finish, I asked the students to jot down their reflections on what we'd done. These are some of their comments:

'At the beginning I thought it would be a bit silly, but I learnt that I needed to concentrate more on the play and it was a change to be outside in the fresh air.'

'However pointless this lesson appeared to be, upon reflection links were made that helped me understand the play better. It was also philosophically eye-opening.'

'I loved this lesson! I enjoyed the hula hooping challenge. I like role-playing but only in a small group of friends, so that was fine. And I caught some sun – yay!'

'I thought the lesson was refreshing and new. It helped gain a different way of learning. However, I hate hula hoops – use footballs instead.'

Are the success criteria clear?

Success criteria are about confidence. Students need to know when they have arrived at the learning destination. If you haven't discussed how they can successfully navigate your objective then things are going to come unstuck later on in the lesson and it will be deuced difficult to establish what they've learnt.

Success criteria are an absolute must; without them students will struggle to do what you want and they will not be able to peer- or self-assess the work they produce. If the objective tells them *what* they're learning, success criteria tell them *how*.

Some people refer to this as WILF (What I'm looking For) and that's fine too, as long as what you come up with:

■ Allows students to make progress.

■ Is straightforward for students to use when assessing their work.

■ Is based on Assessing Pupils' Progress (APP) or GCSE mark schemes.

■ Is produced in collaboration with students.

Ideally, what we want are success criteria which move students from surface to deep understanding. SOLO is the perfect tool to help students progress from having an idea, to lots of ideas, to relating ideas to each other, to extending these ideas into fabulous new landscapes. The first two levels are about surface understanding and the last two are all about deep understanding.

Here's an example:[12]

SOLO level	Learning objective	Success criteria
Uni-/multi-structural	Know a range of rhetorical techniques	I can name one or more rhetorical techniques
Relational	Understand how these techniques can be used to create effects	I can explain how these techniques affect the reader

---

12. These have been adapted from ideas in Steve Martin's *Using SOLO as a Framework for Teaching: A Case Study in Maximising Achievement in Science* (Essential Resources, 2011).

Extended abstract	Be able to use these techniques to create a range of linguistic effects	I can use these techniques in a range of different contexts to provoke a variety of reader responses

Presented with something like this students can see how to move from applying their knowledge base to creating something of worth. The more they know, the more they can analyse and the better they can create or theorise.

Is the learning real?

This is connected to the idea of sharing the big picture (see page 36). It's not enough for us to simply say, 'Now then boys and girls, today we are going to learn about similes.' A reasonable response to this statement might be to ask, what's the point of learning about similes? Or apostrophes? Or Shakespearean comedy? If the best we've got to offer is 'Because I said so' or 'Because it's in the exam' then we're making our lives much more difficult than they need be. Two buzzy acronyms that have been bandied about to the extent that even Ofsted have heard of them are WIIFM (What's In It For Me) and CITV (Connect Into Their Values). These are not educational radio and TV stations but reminders that we ought to be offering students a decent reason for learning the things we're insisting they learn.

Let's imagine you want to convince a class that there is a rationale for knowing what a simile is and how to use one. You will first need to give some thought to the real reasons why writers use them and then allow students to discover for themselves how a well-chosen simile can transform a piece of writing.

So how about trying this? Stride purposefully into the room and, without a word, begin drawing a face on the board. Draw an arrow next to the head and write, 'Head like an egg'. Turn to the class to see their reaction. Offer them the pen. Don't worry if they don't get it yet; continue by labelling the eye with 'Eye like a crater'. Sooner or later they will begin to join in and end up sputtering with delighted laughter at all the hilarious comparisons they make.[13]

How much better is this than waltzing in with the question, 'So, can anyone tell me what a simile is?' Those inclined to dismiss discovery learning as nonsense need look no further. The power of students discovering for themselves the point of a simile (or apostrophe, or subordinate clause, or whatever) is much more likely to be memorable than their teacher just telling them.

We've all encountered the moaning and beating of chests when it's announced that the next topic will be a Shakespeare play or poetry. 'What's the point?' they wail. 'When will I ever need this stuff?' And they've got a point. A lot of what we want students to read and enjoy can seem irrelevant, espe-

---

13. See Trevor Wright, *How To Be A Brilliant English Teacher* (Routledge, 2005), p. 66.

cially the old stuff. The trick is to make it seem less alien and more approachable and beautiful for its own sake.

It's very easy to be sniffy about what kids are interested in and know about. But if we can make meaningful connections between the pop twaddle they're so passionate about and the high culture we want them to fall in love with (or at least consent to sit still and learn about) then we're so much more likely to achieve our ends. We need to design activities that use real-life examples so that students can immediately see the relevance of whatever they're doing.

Here are some simple examples:

- When teaching persuasive writing get students to research a real problem and then write to an actual person. This can be as easy as writing a letter on school uniform to the head teacher, or as ambitious as writing to the Secretary of State about education policy. Anyone who's ever tried this will know the power of reading a reply typed on headed paper.

- Wherever possible get real experts to discuss students' work. Skype is a fantastic tool for this and makes author visits much cheaper and easier to manage.

- Publish students' writing using online tools such as Lulu[14] – having your very own printed book is enormously motivational.

- Get students to set up their own blogs and link these to a class blog. As soon as they realise that other people

---

14. See http://www.lulu.com/gb/.

are reading (and maybe commenting) on their work they'll make much more effort to ensure it is properly spelt and punctuated.

- Discuss good quality newspaper articles on that day's news – maybe even get them to comment on opinion pieces on the internet.

- The local media is always desperate to fill space and will be only too pleased to visit your classroom if you're doing something a little out of the ordinary. Students will be delighted to see themselves and their friends in the local newspaper or on TV and will take the activity much more seriously. Or if you want to go national, sign up for BBC School Report.[15]

---

15. This event happens every March and is an amazing way to motivate students as they build up to the big day. See http://www.bbc.co.uk/schoolreport/.

Chapter 3
During the Lesson

We're on our way. The learning is happening magically all around us and, ideally, you need to be free to have a chat with the students or whoever is observing. The inspector will love it if you are able to not only give them a copy of your lesson plan but also discuss what's going on in the room while the students just get on with whatever exciting activity you've placed before them. The rule of thumb here is that the students should be working independently for about 80% of the lesson. This also gives you the opportunity to take control of the observation and point your interlocutor at the wonders they might otherwise miss.

Clearly, while you're busy glad-handing and hobnobbing, you still need to keep a weather eye on what's occurring. Once again we have our handy checklist of questions to keep us on task.

Is the teaching well paced?

It's important to remember that well paced is not the same as fast paced and is markedly different from furiously paced.

The ideal learning state combines high challenge with low stress.[1] Here is the perfectly paced lesson represented as a graph:

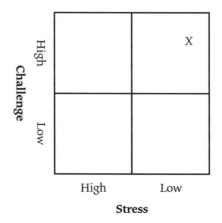

Mihaly Csikszentmihalyi calls this the 'flow' state where stress is low enough that students aren't unduly pressured and agitated but the work they're doing is challenging enough not to be dull.[2]

You know when the class are involved in learning which occupies the top right box. They say things like, 'Can we just finish ...?' or 'That lesson flew by' and you have to shove

---

1. Ian Gilbert, *Essential Motivation in the Classroom* (Routledge Falmer, 2002), p. 40.
2. Mihaly Csikszentmihalyi, *Flow: The Psychology of Optimal Experience* (Harper and Row, 1990).

them bodily out of the room so that you can welcome your next class of eager young minds.

I have this graph up in my room and use it to encourage students to reflect on how they're feeling about their learning. Obviously this might be useful to them, but mainly it's a great help to me to get feedback on where they are and how the lesson is going.

Another hallmark of a well-paced lesson is how transitions are handled. Transitions are those bits of reflection and review that you wedge in-between the lovingly prepared learning activities. If an inspector walks in, make sure you take the time to ask students to reflect on the progress made so far.

Does the teaching hold learners' interests?

As you're no doubt aware, Ofsted inspectors are generally none too keen on what has become known as 'teacher talk'. In order to let students make progress we need to shut up and let the students do some work. But before this can happen we have to do some teaching.

There is definitely a time and place for you to give clear instructions and model how tasks should be completed. This is 'direct instruction' and can be summarised as:

In a nutshell: The teacher decides the learning intentions and success criteria, makes them transparent to the students, demonstrates them by modelling, evaluates if they understand what they have been told by checking for understanding, and re-telling them what they have been told by tying it all together with closure.[3]

So, the problem is that much vaunted difference between *teaching* and *learning*. Maybe Ofsted in their wisdom are aware of the need for knowledge to stick around for longer than 20 minutes.

Research reveals that students learn better when they can self-select or self-generate activities.[4] This means that they need to work in groups and have choice and opportunities to interact with each other. If they don't have these opportunities they'll still do it, but in a way that teachers won't be able to monitor and misinformation can then abound.

Much of what students know is bound up in their peer culture. By varying teaching approaches we can affect the social standing of the students we teach. If we only ever provide traditional academic routes to learning them the 'most able' will have all the power and the 'least able' will quickly, and rightly, become disaffected.

Learning should be a balance between finding out information from a trusted source (the teacher) and discovering it for yourself. I often acquire new ideas from reading books like this one, but it's not until I work out ways to apply these ideas in the classroom that they become part of my teaching arsenal.

---

3. John Hattie, *Visible Learning: A Synthesis of Over 800 Meta-Analyses Relating to Achievement* (Routledge, 2009), p. 206.
4. Graham Nuthall, *The Hidden Lives of Learners* (NZCER Press, 2007), p. 156.

Does the teaching meet a range of learning styles?

Whilst no one still seriously claims that people possess one preferred 'learning style' in which they must be taught or else their ability to learn will be severely impaired, there is disagreement over whether children sometimes *prefer* to *learn* in a particular *style*. What we want is variety.

In writing we want varied punctuation, varied paragraphing, varied sentences and so on. As variety is the spice of life it would be poor practice not to include a broad range of visual, auditory and kinaesthetic teaching approaches. Not because it's the only way to get students to learn but because it would be extremely dull not to. Most teachers would agree that serving up the same old same old isn't a great way of connecting with young minds. It behoves us to vary the way we deliver our lessons.

Lessons that get students out of their seats and wandering around can look great, but we also need to make sure that they are versed in the art of sitting still and writing for extended periods. There's no doubt that many students prefer an active approach to learning but we need to balance this with instilling in them the skills and dispositions needed to succeed in more passive environments.

Does the teaching meet a range of abilities?

It's our old friend differentiation again. We've already dealt with most of the issues in Chapter 1, but it's worth monitoring to ensure that whatever you've planned actually happens.

Let's consider how we could show students how to achieve those A/A* skills of analysing and evaluating. You've probably encountered something like the Grade Ladder before; it can be very useful for helping students understand the skills required to perform at different grades.

Grade Ladder

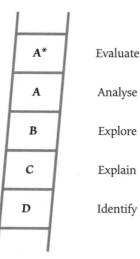

A*	Evaluate
A	Analyse
B	Explore
C	Explain
D	Identify

So, to *identify*, students have to be able to give an opinion and support it with textual evidence.

To *explain*, they have to show they understand the relationship between their point and their evidence. (It is important to specifically teach the use of the word 'because' to ensure this happens.)

Students could demonstrate their ability to *explore* by giving alternative explanations – tentative language becomes important here (It *could* mean ..., but it *might* also suggest ...).

To *analyse* students have to make links and connections with specific details. I encourage them to focus on a word or phrase and try to show what it makes them think about or feel.

Finally, to *evaluate* students have to say how and why a particular technique is effective.

These last two cause the most uncertainty and you may finding Zooming In and Out helpful.[5] Ask students to think about camera shots and how films are put together. When filmmakers zoom in they get us to focus on tiny details and when they zoom out they reveal the big picture. Students have no trouble grasping that analysing is like using an extreme close-up and that evaluating is like using a wide or establishing shot.

---

5. I'm not exactly sure who deserves the credit for the initial idea, but I wouldn't have developed zooming in and out without the help of Liz Winsborough and Rosie Sisson.

Does the teaching actively engage learners in the learning process?

'Engagement' is another one of those trendy buzzwords which Ofsted has obviously become aware of. But all too often engagement can be read as longhand for 'fun'. Now, I've got nothing against learning being enjoyable, but engagement is just a means to an end; in this case the end is the 'learning process'.

Equally important is the idea of 'attention'. When teaching students to structure non-fiction texts I make a point of demonstrating that there's little point in saying anything without the attention of one's audience. Hopefully I have yours. If not, what's the point?

We gain attention with the use of rhetorical questions and direct address. Here is my non-fiction text structure flow chart which, I hope, illustrates the point as well as providing a potentially useful teaching resource.

Using SOLO to engage students in the learning process

The marvellous Lisa Jane Ashes shows how SOLO can also be applied to writing tasks:[6]

1. **Uni-structural.** A new genre, audience or task for their writing purpose.

---

6. A big thank you to Lisa Jane Ashes for this material sourced from her amazing blog: http://lisajaneashes.edublogs.org/2012/01/11/using-solo-in-writing-tasks/.

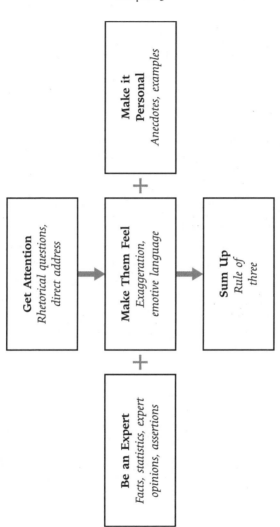

2. **Multi-structural.** Research similar texts and their conventions; explore vocabulary choices – what works and what doesn't; explore different types of sentence for their effect within this type of work as well as exploring mood, tone and composition; explore possible content choices for their work.

3. **Relational.** Students apply their exploration to the creation of a whole text, relating their collated ideas within paragraphs to create a coherent whole.

4. **Extended abstract.** Using the structure created in their relational planning, students make their text unique.

Students need to be aware of the purpose of each step of the planning process so that they are able to recreate it by themselves in controlled conditions. The uni-structural phase of planning consists of a title or central idea. This is what sparks the search for multi-structural knowledge and will be at the heart of everything they are about to do.

Uni-structural phase of planning

"You Dont Know Me"
* Article arguing against the way teenagers are portrayed in the media

The multi-structural phase begins with researching similar writing and exploring examples for composition and effect. Students use questions to gain a deeper understanding of biased arguments such as:

■ What are the conventions of this writing type?

■ Are there any language features that are always/never used?

■ What tone does the writing have?

■ Does anything vary depending on purpose or audience or is the recipe always the same?

Students then explore sentence composition, punctuation usage and anything else that helps them to recognise what works in this genre of writing. They record their findings on their planning sheet in order to keep track of their progress.

Multi-structural phase of planning

As part of their multi-structural research, pupils begin to form ideas about the content they might include in their own writing and then make sense of these ideas by creating a logical order to their topics and adding this to their plan.

Relational phase of planning

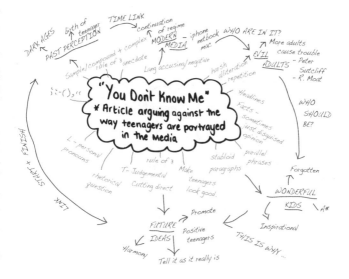

Working out how to structure ideas is the essence of the relational level of thinking. Students relate their research and understanding to the creation of the whole text. If they've amassed enough multi-structural knowledge, they should have little difficulty in creating a piece of work which conforms to the genre conventions they've researched.

Once pupils are happy with the overall structure and direction of their work, they can consider how to make their writing original or unique. Using an extended metaphor is an excellent way to develop an original viewpoint. Although it doesn't work in all genres of writing, it is a good place to start for getting pupils to see how something plodding and pedestrian can start to shine with some simple changes.

Extended abstract phase of planning

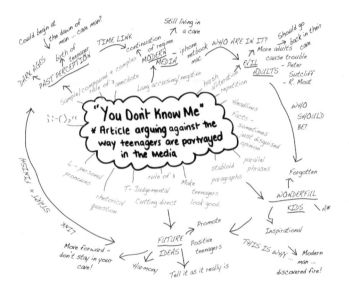

Here's an example of a student's writing using this method:

Why don't you know me? You see me as a loud, obnoxious and aggressive teenager; why is this? The media, that's why. The media is like a Venus flytrap, pretty and innocent, until you get too close. If you are caught within its flower, you could find your-

self being crushed with lies, just like the youth of today; can't you see that this poisonous weed needs to be stopped?

This student began with a basic paragraph plan and then replaced the media with the idea of a poisonous plant to create a distinct and polished piece of writing.

With a little thought this process can be adapted to help students plan any sort of extended writing task.

Are learners given clear information and guidance throughout the lesson?

There is another fine line to tread here. Too much information and guidance and you're guilty of spoon-feeding. Too little and the learning stalls, hands go up, heads go down and you start sweating. Not good.

Here are some techniques you could experiment with to promote independent learning:

- **Modelled examples.** Give them a handout with an example of what you're looking for. Ideally something which can't be copied but which has enough to guide them towards whatever it is you want, without them having to ask for further clarification.
- **Three before me.** Students are required to have asked three other people in class who were paying attention before they come crawling, cap in hand, to the teacher.

■ **Question tokens.** Students are given a piece of card which entitles them to one question only. When they pop up their hands ask, 'Are you sure you want to use your question up on this?'

■ **Reflections board.** I have a display board in my classroom dedicated to students' questions and reflections. They have access to (a set number of) sticky notes and can slap on a comment whenever they feel sufficiently moved. My end of the bargain is to collect these up and address anything pertinent at particular points during the lesson.

■ **Thought stems.** Another display board is dedicated to common sentence stems to get them writing instead of pleading, 'But Sir, how can I start?' I've taught them how to use these and usually a nod in their general direction is sufficient to generate a reluctantly accepting sigh.

Is there any paired or group collaborative work?

Like it or not, group work has to happen in English lessons. For one thing there's the specific need to assess students' ability to be able to discuss topics together as part of the speaking and listening strand of the English curriculum, but perhaps more importantly there's the fact that children learn best in groups.

The word/s ... makes me think/ feel ... because ...

This is effective/ successful because ...

This might also suggest ... because ...

The writer's intention is ...

This shows or suggests or implies ... because ...

If we expect students to remember all the important stuff they need to know, let alone be doing anything useful with it, they need to actively participate in the acquisition of said knowledge through carefully crafted collaborative tasks that enable them to discuss, experiment with and apply new concepts.

Working in groups doesn't make for more creative ideas, but it does provide a safe environment for students to experiment and fail and try again without worrying about the ridicule of the whole class. Group work shouldn't be about coming up with new ideas. Rather it should be about learning stuff deep down in your soul. Working for knowledge is so much more effective than having it proffered on a spoon. Also, it's much easier to check their understanding. You can listen in to their chatter and redirect or question where appropriate.

I'm not for a moment suggesting that this is the only way to teach or that students should always work in groups, but it is one way of providing the variety we mentioned earlier.

Ways to make group work work

■ **Clear roles and responsibilities for all students.** For some students their mission in life is to find ways to avoid doing the work you set them and group work can provide all sorts of opportunities for them to indulge this tendency. If we give everyone in the group a different role and provide them with clear responsibilities these opportunities will be lessened. This does require some thought though. Try to avoid 'boring' jobs like scribe. No one wants to be forced to do all the writing and this can result in vulnerable students being bullied into doing all the work. Instead have exciting roles like 'forensic pathologist' and give them fascinating things to do which would be the envy of everyone else in the group if they didn't have equally exciting and purposeful roles.

- **Student observers.** I call these guys 'learning spies' and their brief is to watch what everyone else is up to and report back. I train them to try to restrict themselves to factual observations and then confront groups with comments like, 'I noticed that you're all sitting under the desk laughing like hyenas. Can you interpret that for me?' This idea is discussed in more detail on page 93.

- **Home/expert groups.** This is my absolute favourite way to teach. Students start in their home groups and are told that they will need to absorb and utilise some wonderful new information. This subject matter is then divided into five discrete parts and students are then moved into expert groups to work on one of these five bits. Each member of the expert group is then responsible for taking back whatever they learn to their home group, which then has to synthesise the entirety of the material. Everyone is required to work at all times, otherwise the home groups will be unable to complete their challenge and the miscreant responsible for this failure can be publicly lambasted.

■ **Short focused group tasks.** Why do group challenges have to take so long? I'm sure there's some sort of equation you could apply to the fact that a group task expands to fill the time you give students to complete it. Often they will produce as much, if not more, if you give them less time than they think they need. Be aware of the 'flow' of the activity so as not to agitate the students into a state of frozen shock and all will be well.

Is questioning used effectively?

Hands up who likes asking questions? Questioning is an essential part of helping students to make progress, but only if it causes thinking or elicits evidence that informs our teaching. And the problem with asking questions is that while there are some students who know how to make the system work for them and actively participate in lessons, because that they way they'll learn more, there are those who don't. Dylan Wiliam claims that the students who are sufficiently engaged to put up their hands and answer everything we ask them are 'actually getting smarter. Their IQs actually go up.'[7] Now, I can't vouch for the research on this but if it's true, by allowing some students not to participate we're making the achievement gap bigger. Not good.

A solution to this is to use a randomised name generator. You can go low tech by writing students' names onto lolly

---

7. Dylan Wiliam speaking in *The Classroom Experiment*, BBC2, 27 and 28 September 2010 [TV series].

sticks à la Dylan Wiliam, or you can experiment with various free web-based teaching tools like Triptico.[8]

Once we've got students to actually answer a question we need to give them enough time to think. We've known for ages that if you allow more time for students to reply to your questions, more thoughtful answers will be offered in response. Typically we only allow 1 second for students to answer a question.[9] With this kind of pressure it's no wonder that 75% of students avoid risking potential humiliation. Ideally we should allow something in the region of 4 seconds thinking time. Now that could be 4 seconds of tumbleweed or you could give the students the chance to discuss possible answers and maybe even jot down a few possibilities. Sometimes giving them a specific number of answers to come up with (five is my favourite) means that when we ask students for their answer they'll have at least something to contribute.

But what sort of questions should we be asking? *Hinge* questions are a hugely useful diagnostic tool which provide data on students' understanding and allow you to make real-time decisions about the direction of your teaching without wast-

---

8. Triptico is a suite of useful tools designed by David Riley, an English teacher, for English teachers. It's available as a free download from http://www.triptico.co.uk/.

9. See Mary Budd Rowe, 'Wait Time: Slowing Down May Be a Way of Speeding Up!', *Journal of Teacher Education* 37(1) (1986), 43–50.

ing anybody's time. Here are some pointers on hinge questions:

- It should be based on *the* important concept in a lesson that is critical for students to understand before you move on in the lesson.
- The question should fall about midway during the lesson.
- Every student must respond to the question within 2 minutes.
- You must be able to collect and interpret the responses from all students in 30 seconds.
- You need to decide in advance how many students you need to get the right answer – 20–80% depending on how important the question is.[10]

All this means that you won't have time to get students to explain their answers. This feels unnatural for an English teacher – we always want to know *why* – but the point here is to check understanding, work out whether you need to recap or change direction and then get a move on.

To make this work you'll need to make the questions multiple choice and have access to an essential piece of English teaching kit: a set of mini-whiteboards or some clever, ed-tech equivalent.

---

10. The suggestion is that if the question is crucial for students to make progress, then at least 80% need to be answering it correctly in order for you to move on. If the question will be answered later and opportunities for clearing up misunderstandings have already been planned into the lesson then this percentage could be as low as 20%. Popham, J., *Transformative Assessment*.

Here are a couple of examples:

Where is the verb in this sentence?

A lion roared ferociously at me.
  ↑   ↑   ↑   ↑

  A   B   C   D

Which of these is alliteration?

A. *The hot sun glared down.*

B. *Sweetly smiling sunshine.*

C. *Night fell suddenly.*

D. *The tree stooped in despair.*

The second example highlights the importance of asking the right question. What would happen if instead the question were: 'Which of these is an example of personification?' I'll tell you what would happen: we'd end up bogged down in a teacher-led discussion in which everyone, except for the keeners at the front, is thoroughly bored.

A good hinge question needs a lot of careful thought and planning: they won't just happen. But there's no hiding with the mini-whiteboard there to expose every teensy misapprehension so that you can swoop, falcon-like, and restore the beatific smile of understanding to even the most perennially confused child.

Lessons are much richer if the focus of questions is moved away from testing students' knowledge of facts to exploring their understanding. We should know from our thinking about SOLO that deep understanding depends upon students' knowledge base: they need to know stuff before they can think about it. At this point you can safely ask the thought-provoking, open-ended questions that will have the inspector purring happily in the corner.

Question Formulation Technique

Asking well-designed questions is an excellent thing to be doing and we should absolutely be doing it. But it's worth reflecting on the fact that we ask an awful lot of questions. Don't get me wrong, effective questioning is the key to many successful learning experiences and underpins assessment for learning, but why is it always *us* asking the questions?

It stands to reason that if a student creates their own question they are more likely to take ownership of it and actually *want* to answer it. It's interesting to consider that students can learn more from asking questions than they can from answering them.

Enter the Question Formulation Technique. QTF is the brainchild of the Right Question Institute and suggests four essential rules for producing your own questions:[11]

---

11. See Dan Rothstein and Luz Santana, 'Teaching Students to Ask Their Own Questions: One Small Change Can Yield Big Results', *Harvard Education Letter* 27(5) (2011). Available at http://www.hepg.org/hel/article/507/.

Chapter 3

1. **Ask as many questions as you can**
   ■ Don't stop to discuss, judge or answer the questions.
   ■ Write down every question exactly as it is stated.
   ■ Change any statement into a question.

2. **Improve your questions**
   ■ Categorise the questions as closed or open ended.
   ■ Name the advantages and disadvantages of each type of question.
   ■ Change questions from one type to another.

3. **Prioritise the questions**
   ■ Choose your three most important questions.
   ■ Why did you choose these three as the most important?

4. **Next steps**
   ■ How are you going to use your questions?

We all want students who have the confidence to learn independently, take risks and who see failure as an opportunity for further growth and development. Getting students to ask interesting questions would seem to slot in well.

Here's a lesson on characterisation in Steinbeck's *Of Mice and Men* which focuses on getting students to come up with good quality questions. The class were preparing for a speaking and listening assessment by role-playing the development of characters' relationships in section 3 (the dog-shooting,

85

hand-crushing bit). The first part of the plan was to arrange the class into home groups and share details about their intended role-play.

From there, they moved into expert groups: one for each of the five main characters they were to write about. Step 1 was to come up with as many questions as possible about their character on some big paper (I *love* big paper!) without criticism, quality control or discussion.

Step 1

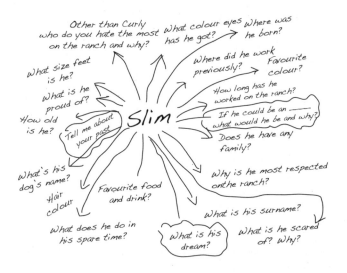

They then had to sort their questions into categories (step 2) and think about the characteristics of 'good' questions. I gave them a bit of direction here and suggested they think about open/closed and factual/conceptual questions. I had thought they might find this tricky but was pleased to find myself proved wrong yet again.

Step 2

These are 'good' questions

To what extent is she meant to be representative of all women?

What might have happened if Lennie hadn't killed her?

Curley's Wife

Why do the ranch workers feel so threatened by her?

How important is she to the story?

Why didn't Steinbeck give Curley's wife a name?

The transition between steps 2 and 3 seemed to occur almost seamlessly as categorising led them naturally into making decisions about 'good' and 'bad' questions. Each group arrived at their three 'best' questions quickly and were eager to share with other groups.

Step 3

George
- *Why does he want Lennie to stay with him?*
- *Why doesn't he want Lennie to speak?*
- *Does Lennie hinder George? And why?*

- *Why does he always play cards?*
- *Why does he like Lennie?*   - *Does George have a soft side?*
- *What are George's emotions?*
- *Is George always angry?*
- *Is Lennie afraid of George?*   - *Where's George from?*
- *Is George scared of anyone?*   *Does George*
- *Why won't George let Lennie have pets?*   *have other feelings*
- *Is George nasty or nice?*   *for Lennie?*
- *Does George dislike dogs or mice?*
- *Is George a social person?*
- *What is George's favourite card game?*
- *Why doesn't George want Lennie hanging around women?*

Finally, we reshuffled back into home groups and got on with planning for the speaking and listening assessment (step 4). When we came to review the learning and consider the advantages of asking rather than answering questions, students made comments like:

'It makes you think deeper ...'

'I had to consider more things than usual.'

'We didn't waste time writing answers that we already knew.'

This is a far better way for students to engage with Steinbeck's characters than simply reading about them and then having a discussion. The impact is certainly worth the minimal effort: the students do all the work and you get to wander around encouraging, occasionally redirecting, and having quality learning conversations about your observations.

Are all learners actively involved?

Ask students to reflect on what they've done so far and how they've done it. The following questions might be useful:

- Has any of the lesson so far been about you?
- What connections have you made?
- How do you feel about the lesson?
- How have you got involved in the lesson?
- What should you do to further your thinking?
- What breakthroughs have you made?
- What do you want to know more about?
- What are you currently thinking about?

Again, the idea is for students to select a question from the list and then consider their answer. Used in combination with some sort of randomisation device (e.g. lolly sticks) you have a nifty way of demonstrating that everyone is involved and expected to participate in the learning.

Another excellent strategy for involving the whole class is our old friend the hinge question (see page 45). Both of these ideas will demonstrate to the inspector that you are able to engage every single student in the room.

Is clear feedback given on progress?

A lot of the feedback we give students is too little, too late; too vague and too impersonal. It shouldn't come as a surprise to hear that effective feedback needs to relate to your learning objective. A lot of the feedback students are given (especially by English teachers) seems to focus on presentation, punctuation, spelling, the quantity of writing and effort. All these are important, but if they have nothing to do with your learning objective then it's unfair to bang on about them.

Ask yourself, does your feedback:

- Let students know what they're doing well?
- Give clear guidance on what needs to be improved?
- Provide the next steps in learning and how students can take them?

Whether it's written or verbal, good feedback should take the form of a conversation. Ideally, these conversations will cover the following ground:

- What is your goal?
- What progress are you making?

■ What else do you need to do?

Giving immediate verbal feedback or brief written comments while students are working promotes more effective learning. Get students to leave spaces in their books for you to write prompts to help improve their work. These remarks can take different forms:

■ Reminder: Say more about ...

■ Question: Can you describe how ...?

■ Example: Give an example to show what you are saying.

A word to the wise: feedback is not the same as praise. Praise is great, but it needs to be realistic. Regular, excessive praise often does more harm than good, leading to delusion or even frustration and resentment – it can help to foster those pesky fixed mindsets about ability. For feedback to be effective it needs to be separate from praise. Saying, 'Well done, you've tried really hard but you need to remember that commas go before the main clause' isn't going to work. Students will either be confused (did they do well or not?) or they'll not hear the feedback.

Observing learning

One of the main reasons for organising activities so that students work together without the need for direct supervision from you the whole time is so that you can circulate and engage in quality learning conversations and provide effective feedback. Your role is to observe the learning and record your observations without making any kind of judgement. Sounds pretty straightforward, but this can be a radical approach.

The trick is to set up group tasks with clear success criteria and teams in which all students have a clear area of responsibility; then give them the freedom to approach the tasks without interference. This doesn't need to involve the teacher 'sitting in', which can be pretty nerve-wracking, especially when watching a group 'getting it wrong'.

Once students start work all you have to do is circulate and scribble observations on the board to discuss later; other notes could be added to the group's table with no further comment. Observations should be along the lines of:

- I notice that no one is speaking.
- I heard you mention ...
- I saw you do ...

At first students will be overwhelmed with curiosity about what you're writing and this can impact on their group dynamics, but like anything else they'll soon get used to your antics.

At the end of the lesson, ask students to reflect on your observations and interpret them. If you've taken photos, display them and ask students to explain what was happening. What they say is often surprising. One student responded to my observation, 'I notice you have your headphones in your ears,' with an explanation about how they weren't plugged in and that having them in helped to block out distractions.

This was a revelation: in the past I would, at the very least, have told him to take them out and might even have confiscated them. Maybe I'm gullible, but I believed him.

The point of all this is that it gives students an opportunity to take responsibility for interpreting their own actions. This has always been the teacher's preserve and our judgement usually determines the success or failure of the work students do.

Learning spies

Learning spies are basically my rebranding of student observers and are a superb way of freeing you up to be able to give feedback. Quite simply, instead of me having to keep an eye on what students working in teams get up to, the spies do it. They get a pro forma to keep track of what they see, hear and the group interactions they observe. Use Critical Skills teams with clearly defined roles and responsibilities for all and set up challenges that cannot be completed without the active participation of all concerned.[12]

The role of the spy is much more important than mere behaviour management. If they are well trained they can become a powerful and immediate way to provide fantastic formative assessment for their peers to act upon.

This leaves you free to wander around and get a feel for the progress learners are making and collect 'evidence' of what

---

12. The Critical Skills Program is a methodology for getting students to work successfully in teams. See http://www.antiochne.edu/acsr/criticalskills/.

you've observed. At various points during lessons, you should have one-to-one chats with learners during which you confront them with this evidence and ask them to interpret it. At other times you could take a team member aside for a chat about how they feel their team is getting on. For example: Is the team leader doing a good job? How are they managing their own role?

The spies should be doing the same thing. They will have been busily scribbling down key interactions and their effects as well as making decisions about how they will offer feedback. They're empowered to have 'learning chats' with their teammates and ask them to interpret their observations. Asking questions like this is much more powerful than me (or the spies) simply saying, 'You weren't on task.' You have to give students the benefit of the doubt. Who knows, maybe the student resting their head on the desk isn't asleep – maybe they're thinking. The point is that if you (or a spy) say, 'I noticed you had your head on the desk, can you tell me why?' then we sometimes get some interesting and surprising answers.

What do the spies get out of it? Well, often they'll have actually learnt more through watching others struggling to get to grips with something than if they had been doing the struggling themselves. They also say that they end up working at least as hard, if not harder, than those they're observing.

At the end of the lesson, and at strategic points throughout, spies are required to lead a plenary where they feed back to their groups about the skills and dispositions they have been observing and then chair a discussion about the group's interpretation.

It might not come as a surprise that students vie for the opportunity to spy on their peers, but might it surprise you to know that they clamour equally as much after experiencing how hard they have to work?

Is pupil knowledge and understanding increased?

The best way to show that you're increasing knowledge and understanding is to head towards what is commonly referred to as 'deep' learning. This is knowledge that transfers from students' working memories into their long-term memories.

As we've already seen, students understand new ideas by relating them to old ideas. If their knowledge is too shallow they won't have a solid base from which to make connections to prior knowledge. Students are more likely to remember learning if they 'make their own sense of what they are learning, and relate it to what they know'.[13]

As a teacher you will possess broad experience and deep knowledge of a wide variety of topics, which will mean you

---

13. See Geoff Petty, *Evidence-Based Teaching: A Practical Approach*, 2nd edn (Nelson Thornes, 2009).

are usually pretty good at transferring what you know from one sphere to another. Not so students. The fact that they know less across the board makes it much harder for them to apply what they've learnt about abstract concepts to other areas. Daniel Willingham's advice to teachers is as follows:[14]

■ Provide examples and get students to compare them.

■ Make deep knowledge the spoken and unspoken emphasis.

■ Accept that shallow knowledge is better than nothing.

Hexagonal learning

Using hexagons is a wonderful way to connect students' multi-structural knowledge base together (see page 97) and make any relationships visible.[15] Why hexagons? Because they've got six sides and when you give a pile of them to kids their natural response is to start fitting them together and making connections. You can write whatever you want onto the hexagons or leave them blank for students to fill in. In this very simple example we have some words connected to *Macbeth*:

---

14. Daniel Willingham, *Why Don't Students Like School?* (Jossey-Bass, 2009), pp. 95–97.
15. This is adapted from ideas on Damian Clark's blog: http://invisiblelearning. blogspot.co.uk/.

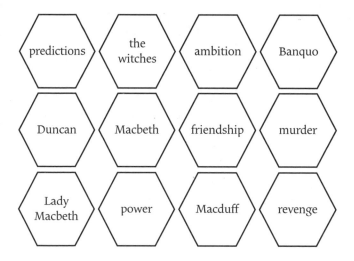

Students use their multi-structural knowledge of the play to show the relationships between the hexagons. Obviously, there's no correct way to do this; the point is that students get to show off their deep understanding by explaining the links they've created.

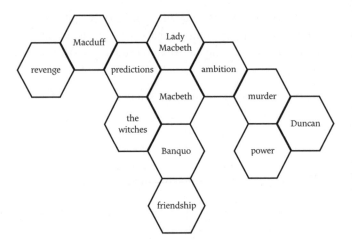

Is the relational understanding different here?

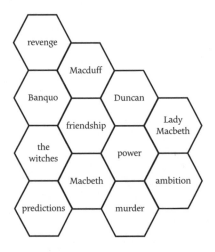

It's almost impossible for students not to start making links, and this practically guarantees that they will demonstrate a relational understanding of whatever topic they're learning about.

To move to the extended abstract, students could explore the intersections and show an appreciation of Shakespeare's intentions. This almost invites abstract questions. For instance, 'How does Shakespeare connect Macbeth with friendship and power?' Or 'Does Shakespeare use Lady Macbeth and Duncan to show different views of power?'

This can work equally well with language analysis. Here's an example comparing the language of Simon Armitage's 'The Manhunt' with Carol Ann Duffy's 'Quickdraw':

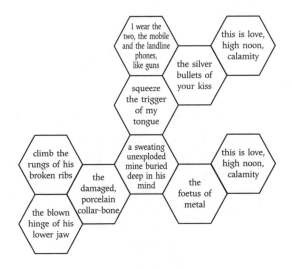

The connections made will depend on how much the students already know about the poems. It makes a great introductory activity when they are encountering these works for the first time. There are some fairly obvious links that can be made and these are a great starting point for getting students to consider the effects of language and to interpret the writers' possible intentions. How about using the cards as a way into answering an abstract question like 'Are love and pain different sides of the same coin?'

The idea of cutting out hundreds of hexagons may seem a little off-putting. One solution is to have a few laminated, wipe-clean sets, but the technically minded amongst you may like to experiment with Think Link (triptico.co.uk).

Is there opportunity for pupils to demonstrate increased knowledge and understanding?

OK, so their brains are bulging with everything they've just learnt; they now need to show what they know and wow the inspector. Which is just as well as there's no way you're going to be able to formatively assess their progress unless they've done some actual work.

Whilst we want our lessons to be enjoyable it's also crucial to foster an understanding that success is based on the ability to pull out one's finger and work hard. You see, it's fairly easy to settle for a low grade. You don't have work very hard to coast. But getting an A*? That would require blood, sweat and tears. It might be uncomfortable. It would be a damn sight easier not to try! It's a fairly standard fixed mindset response to see effort as evidence of failure.

Anyone can be better than they currently are; anyone can improve. Sadly though, it requires effort. It's not easy.

So with all this hard work done, we need to ensure that there are ample opportunities for students to strut their stuff and show off what they've accomplished. A simple rule of thumb is that during the lesson students should be working independently for 60-80% of the time. This means you have to shut up and let them do stuff. But that's no problem because you'll be busy giving feedback on all the amazing learning you've provoked.

Are reading and writing skills developed?

Writing skills

We often get bogged down with content. When teaching writing we tend to faff about with genre conventions and vocabulary instead of getting to grips with the mechanics of sentence structure and punctuation. But is this the correct approach?

Here are two points to consider:

1. Lots of English teachers are uncomfortable with teaching grammar and are keenly aware of their own lack of knowledge.

2. Knowledge is power. And ignorance is not bliss. If students are confused about basics like what a sentence is and how it works then they are at a serious disadvantage. Whilst able readers and writers seem to acquire an instinctive understanding of how grammar 'feels' without being clear about any of the rules, most others flounder.

This is a good reason to suggest that the perfect English lesson ought to contain a good-sized portion of spelling, punctuation and grammar. This is not an argument for dry, boring lessons. Instead try creative and engaging ways to get students practising basic literacy skills.

These skills often follow rules which can be investigated and tested. For instance, most students seem to be of the opinion that you put a comma where you draw breath. Instead of simply attempting to beat this misconception out of them, get them to analyse texts to see if they can work out a better rule for how commas are used. Or maybe get them to compare a text in its natural state with one you've doctored so that all the complex sentences begin with subordinate clauses. What will they notice? Not only that comma usage follows clear and understandable rules but that this is also a fantastic way into considering the effects of commas. Let's face it, if they discover these rules for themselves they're much more likely to remember and use them.

Although there are relatively few marks available for spelling and none for handwriting, Ofsted are keen to see these skills being developed in English lessons and comment that

'Marking at best prioritised the identification of broad targets but rarely noted individual errors in spelling and grammar. The result was that many students received no further help with poor handwriting or spelling.'[16] The perfect English lesson will insist that students are asked to learn spelling rules and use phonic charts to establish how to correct mis-spellings. Not all poor handwriting is the result of carelessness but much is. If students are relentlessly made to rewrite work which is poorly presented, or has not been proofread, they will quickly get into good habits.

Kung fu punctuation

One of the most enjoyable ways to teach writing skills is to introduce your classes to the secret art of kung fu punc-tuation.[17] Every piece of punctuation has an accompanying action and sound which will have your students learning in the best wax on, wax off fashion. Phil Beadle describes the process so well in *Could Do Better!* that it seems point-less to attempt to rephrase it:[18]

■ **Full stop:** throw a short, right-handed punch at the air in front of you. Make the noise, Ha!

■ **Comma:** with your right arm bent so that your hand is in front of your face, make a short twisting motion

---

16. Ofsted, *Moving English Forward: Action to Raise Standards in English* (15 March 2012). Ref: 110118. Available at http://www.ofsted.gov.uk/resources/moving-english-forward, p. 27.
17. This idea is based on the work of Ros Wilson, the creator of Big Writing.
18. Phil Beadle, *Could Do Better! Help Your Kid Shine At School* (Doubleday, 2007), p. 43–44.

at the wrist to signify the comma shape. Make the noise, Shi!

- **Semi-colon:** do the full-stop punch, then the comma shape directly underneath it. Make the noises, Ha! Shi!

- **Colon:** follow the full-stop punch immediately with one directly beneath it. Make the noises, Ha! Ha!

- **Question mark:** separate the curly bit into three cutting movements with the hand: one horizontal left to right, one curved around, and one vertical coming from the bottom of the curved one. Then at the bottom of the shape you have just drawn in the air, bung in a full-stop punch. Make the noises, Shi! Shi! Shi! Ha!

- **Exclamation mark:** a long vertical slash, from top to bottom, followed by a full stop. Make the noises, Shiiiiii! Ha!

- **Speech marks:** stand on one leg, extend your arms diagonally to the skies and wiggle your index and middle fingers in an approximation of speech marks. Make the noise, Haeeeee!

- **Apostrophe:** with your right arm fully extended to the air, wiggle your index finger. Flap your tongue up and down to create a blubablubabluba sound.

- **Ellipsis:** three punches along a horizontal line. Make the noises, Ha! Ha! Ha!

■ **Brackets:** using your left hand first, draw a curved convex line in the air; use your right hand to do the opposite motion for the closing bracket. Make the noises, Shi! Shi!

Once these moves have been mastered, you're ready to play. Get the class to form two lines facing each other. Before they begin they must bow formally to their partner to signal respect for the opponent's punctuation skills and make a capital letter sign by holding both hands together to make a rough triangle or a stylised A. With the formalities out of the way, you then read a pre-prepared sentence and the opponents duel to see who can complete the sounds and actions most quickly.

Reading skills

For some reason, reading strategies and guided reading have fallen off the education radar in recent years.[19] Guided reading is based on the practice of reciprocal teaching which research suggests is one of the highest impact strategies we can use.[20]

---

19. Guided reading involves a teacher and a group of around four or six students. Sessions are often focused on objectives to be taught within 20–30 minutes. While guided reading takes place with one group of children, the remaining students are engaged in reading independently so that the teacher is not interrupted while focusing on one group.

20. John Hattie gives reciprocal teaching a whopping effect size of 0.74. See his *Visible Learning: A Synthesis of Over 800 Meta-Analyses Relating to Achievement* (Routledge, 2009), p. 244.

Now, you may want to argue that reading comprehension depends on background knowledge and that teaching generic reading skills won't impact on this. Whilst this is true, it's not the full picture. As with anything, when skills are made explicit students can unpick how they approach a text and are more likely to think about using different strategies when approaching a new, unfamiliar text.

The reading strategies are:

- **Skimming** – reading quickly to get an overview
- **Scanning** – searching for key information
- **Inferring** – using clues to work out meanings
- **Empathising** – seeing events from another's perspective
- **Visualising** – creating an image in your mind
- **Reading backwards and forwards** – making connections
- **Close reading** – zooming in on key words and phrases
- **Questioning** – asking questions about a text
- **Predicting** – making informed guesses

Each of these needs to be explained explicitly and then demonstrated as students read.

Whilst reading a text you should pause at opportune points and ask students which strategies they've used and tell them which ones you were using. Once they've started to get the hang of it you're ready for a spot of guided reading.

At this stage students need to be divided into groups. You can make this as simple or as complicated as you like, but the easiest way to get going is to tell students how far to read in a text and give them a time limit in which to do it. You join one group and get them each to read a few paragraphs aloud in turn. After each student has finished reading you will lead a brief discussion on which strategies were used before continuing.

Guided reading should be a regular feature of all English lessons and the reading strategies need to be the rock on which students' understanding of how they read is built. This also fits in fantastically well with the current vogue for teachers getting out of the way so that learning can happen.

Students also need to be given opportunities to read for pleasure. It's been suggested that 'children as young as 11 should be expected to read 50 books a year as part of a national drive to improve literacy standards'.[21] As English teachers we need to make sure we are modelling a love of reading to our students.

Here are some tips on doing this:

▪ Talk about what you're reading. Read out extracts and get students to discuss what their response is.

▪ Set aside time in lessons for silent reading and use this as an opportunity to chat to students about what they're reading. Try to make these times as relaxing as possible and don't get too stressed by reluctant readers.

---

21. Graeme Paton, 'Michael Gove: Pupils Should Read 50 Books a Year', *Daily Telegraph*, 22 March 2011. Available at http://www.telegraph.co.uk/education/educationnews/8396823/Michael-Gove-pupils-should-read-50-books-a-year.html/.

- Visit the school library and find examples of books your students might enjoy.

- Get students to write reviews of the books they've read and keep a folder of these on tap to tempt others with. You could also try publishing these reviews online and then creating a QR code[22] which could be stuck to the cover of the book.

- Invite authors into lessons to talk about their work or set up a Skype call with them.

- Have a book display in your room and encourage students to borrow (with permission) anything that takes their fancy.

Numeracy

What? In an English lesson? Yes, just as every other teacher is responsible for teaching literacy, so we share the responsibility for numeracy. Here are a couple of suggestions for wedging in a spot of numeracy which will actually help students write better.

- **Think of a number.** Give students some dice and get them to record the results of five throws. Then ask them to choose another five numbers between 7 and 20. This will leave them with a string of numbers such as: 3, 1, 4, 1, 2, 18, 9, 11, 13, 10 – this then needs mixing up so that we arrive at something more like this: 3, 10, 1, 11,

---

22. If you scan a QR (Quick Response) code with a QR reader app on a smart-phone it will take you to a website.

9, 4, 18, 1, 13, 2. Now their job is to produce a short piece of writing (subject and form to be plucked from your head) with these numbers dictating the length of the sentences they must write. This may not produce any prize-winning delights but it will make the students think carefully about their writing and it will force them to vary their sentence length.[23]

■ **SVO.** This is also about sentence structure and the aim is to get students to approach their writing as series of equations. As you know, sentences need to contain a subject (S) and verb (V) and something else, often an object but it's more helpful to refer to it as other (O). It's also useful to teach connectives (C). Once students have learnt these terms, and become familiar with applying them, the fun begins. You could either make up some flash cards or use your projector to display different sentence structures in this form:

SVO   VSO   SVO+SVO   SVO; SVO
CSVO, SVO   SVOCSVO

As above, the students' job is to construct sentences on a chosen topic which fit these structures. You can also use this notation to mark students' writing to demonstrate to them what's wrong with their run-on sentences in a very visual way.[24]

---

23. This idea is adapted from something Phil Beadle came up with in *Could Do Better!*, p. 194.
24. This idea comes from Hannah Thomas (an advanced skills teacher at Priory Community School).

Chapter 4
The End of the Lesson

The best lessons are rounded with a review to remind students what it was they should have learnt. It also allows you to see where they are to assist you in planning for the next lesson. This is, or should be, the best bit. This is where you get to show off just how much progress everyone has made.

The end of your lesson should contain combinations of the following:

■ Review of key points.

■ Giving students opportunities to draw conclusions.

■ Describing when and how the students can use this new information.

■ Previewing future lessons.

■ Exhibiting student learning.

■ Creating a smooth transition from one lesson to the next.

Are the learning objectives reviewed?

The spirit is usually willing but the timekeeping is occasionally weak. The biggest problem for any serious attempt to review learning objectives is lack of time. A good 10 minutes is required to do this properly.

The point is not that at the end of lesson students know whether or not they have learnt what you were expecting them to learn. No, the point is that *you* know whether they learnt it and are in a position to do something about it.

So, whatever you do, make it easy to collect and act on this information. There's little or no point in getting them to tick off whether they've met the objectives – are you *really* going to check these ticks at the end of every lesson? Much better to get students to write down their ruminations on a sticky note and pop it somewhere visible.

If you've used a system like the learning continuum (described in Chapter 2), then you're in prime position to get students to write down exactly where they've got to and what they need to go further. All you need to do now is collect their reflective sticky notes and act on them for the next lesson.

Are questions used to check what learning has taken place?

One way to ensure you're using questions in an interesting way is to finish off with a good list of questions. These might help:

- How are you going to remember this learning?
- What is the key aspect you will remember from this lesson?
- What has this lesson reminded you of?
- Which senses were most important?
- What did you learn that you didn't know before?
- What have you learnt that could be useful elsewhere?
- What have you learnt elsewhere that is like this?
- How will you apply what you have learnt?

Students should choose a question from the list and come up with an answer. This will be a sound basis for discussion on the learning that has (or hasn't) taken place.

Is there feedback from teacher to pupils?

As English teachers we're faced with an extraordinary marking burden. Our students produce a lot of written work and most of it needs to be read carefully rather than given a cursory tick 'n' flick. Marking students' books helps to ensure that they care about the work they produce. I also know that providing formative feedback is the most important intervention that I, as a teacher, can have on my students. There is nothing that will have more impact on their success than good old-fashioned comment-based marking.

No marking? No targets. No targets? No improvement.

No amount of tick 'n' flick, lolly sticks, traffic lights, peer- and self-assessment or parental comment will excuse me from the fact that marking books should be my number one priority and that I should damn well stop making excuses and get on with it.

It's crucial to remind ourselves that formative assessment is *not* marking. Formative assessment is what the marking is *for*. Students showing understanding by displaying red, amber or green cards isn't the point; it's what happens afterwards. And cramming lessons full of peer- and self-assessment is great, but it's what the teachers and students do with the information *after* the peer- and self-assessment happens that is really important.

Assessment for learning *must* consist of the following processes:

■ Establishing where the learners are in their learning.
■ Establishing where they are going.
■ Working out how to get there.

We also need to keep in mind that inspectors are now looking at marking to see if the student has applied the advice over time. You can make this easy to track by highlighting your targets and getting students to copy them into the front of their books. Before starting a new piece of work simply refer them back to their target.

Is there pupil-to-pupil feedback?

One way to utilise pupil-to-pupil feedback is to involve students in the marking process. This takes a deal of training and they require absolutely clear and specific success criteria to make the feedback meaningful. But, with perseverance, students can become excellent peer assessors. The comments they make will be useful as long as they're marking against clear and meaningful success criteria and have an understanding about how to improve work.

There are all sorts of excellent educational reasons why we should be doing this. Not only does it involve students in using and understanding rubrics in a way that will help them move their own work forward, it also provides a useful window into how they are interpreting the success criteria and ensures that students are sharing their work without lengthy and tedious teacher-led feedback sessions. On the whole students enjoy peer-assessment – they don't feel exposed and are inclined to be positive towards the work of others.

The very worst sort of feedback goes along the lines of, 'Well done, you worked really hard but you could make it neater. Lol ;)'. This is not the fault of the students; it's your fault for not showing them how to do it better and giving them the tools to make it meaningful. Meaningful feedback requires clear success criteria. And in order for success criteria to be useful they need to be co-constructed with students or based on mark schemes.

But aren't mark schemes impenetrable wads of edu-drivel that even seasoned teachers are often unclear about? Well, yes, sometimes, but there are some definite pros to using mark schemes with students: chiefly, students have ownership of how their work will be assessed and their progression will be clear and focused on meaningful outcomes.

Because of the language difficulties, students may find it hard to use a mark scheme and will need a good bit of practice applying grade descriptors in order for them to be fully understood. Some might suggest that the best thing to do is to provide 'student friendly' versions but this can do everybody a disservice. Nuanced meaning often gets lost in our attempts to decode the language of rubrics into something that the least literate child in a class can comprehend. Much better to have mark scheme friendly students. Again, this takes some training and perseverance but hopefully you'll arrive at a place where most students have a grasp of where they are and how to make progress to the next level.

Is there evidence of self-assessment?

Although you've got to get peer-assessment right first, self-assessment is ultimately much more important. If we can lead students to the point where they can self-assess an exam essay and say with confidence, 'That's a B that is, Sir', then our work will be done.

The difficulty with self-assessment is that we often have to struggle against a form of dysmorphia which allows many students to look at their work and either screw it up in disgust, toss it in the bin and proclaim it to be rubbish, or, equally alarmingly, to be convinced their shoddy work is far better than it is. Obviously these positions are extremes, but many students find it hard to take a long, hard, detached look, reflect on what's good and what needs to be improved and then set a meaningful target that will be acted on.

Why do they struggle to honestly assess their own work? Well, maybe it's got something to do with society's twin evils: on the one hand, no one likes a show-off and, on the other, if you don't stick up for yourself no one else is going to. There's a big pinch of the fixed mindset in both of these narratives and part of the solution lies in training children who are lacking in self-confidence to either acknowledge that they're wrong or to admit that their efforts have worth. Again, with perseverance and clear parameters, self-assessment can be made to work well.

It's important that students know that their self-assessment will be overseen and checked by you. Not only does this ensure that no one goofs off, it also means that everyone is aware of the clear and meaningful targets against which students can make progress.

Then they need to do it again. And again. This last stage is all too often missed out. What's the point of all that wonderful formative assessment if we don't give the students the immediate opportunity to act on it? If we leave it a few weeks we'll all most likely have forgotten how to do it. They may well groan but they do appreciate it when you can praise them for being able to do whatever it was you taught them.

The same principle underlies my insistence that students proofread and edit their work before handing it in. If you find mistakes which they could and should have spotted, give it back and make them rewrite it. If you are content to do this again and again, proofreading will become second nature.

Is the next lesson previewed?

We've already agreed that it's important to let students know why we're doing what we're doing – they're more likely to remember stuff if they can see how it connects. But don't forget the fact that three is the magic number so we need to provide opportunities for students to encounter new information as often as possible.

Something that's easy to do is to simply tell them at the end of the lesson what they'll be doing next lesson. Even better, don't just tell: make them work it out. Give them some clues, a teaser, something, *anything* to whet their appetites for the learning to come. Remember, we want to give them access to the big picture so they can see how and why the information and skills you're teaching are worth acquiring.

Is the lesson brought to a clear close?

At its most basic, this involves the students packing away in an orderly manner and standing quietly behind their chairs waiting to be dismissed, which is fine. But with the barest hint of imagination the simple act of closing a lesson can become a thing of beauty.

Try using Exit Pass questions which students must answer before they are allowed to leave. Give out a different question to each student on a group of tables at the beginning of the lesson and ask them what they've come up with at the end. The fact that they've had the question all lesson, combined with the knowledge that they'll have to answer it before you'll let them pack up, is enough to prevent all but the most truculent from moaning.

In order to make sure there's time to check everyone's answers, try placing three containers somewhere in the room. Colour-code the pots red, amber and green. Into these pots students will pop a slip of paper with their name on, indicating their level of understanding on today's topic. At the end of the lesson you will have a simple way of checking each student's understanding, enabling you to build this into your next lesson. There are all sorts of ways to tweak this – but the point is that it's easy to use, highly visible and provides a 'safe' way for students to feed back on their learning.

Another way to do this is to hand out sticky notes and ask students to scribble down something using the following prompts:

☺ *I really understood this idea.*

☺ *I have a few questions about ...*

☹ *I don't even know where to start on ...*

Or:

! I am excited about ...

: I'd like to learn more about ...

? A question I have is ...

Or:

▲ *This point is really clear.*

■ *One thing that squares with things I already know is ...*

● *An idea that is still going around in my head is ...*

So there we are: the perfect end to the perfect English lesson.

The Perfect Lesson Checklist

The Perfect Lesson Checklist

 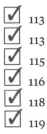

Appendix

A bit more on the SOLO Taxonomy

Of all the pedagogical tips and tricks I've read about, SOLO has had more impact on my teaching and my students' learning than any other. If you search really hard, you'll be able to unearth articles on ways to use SOLO in various subjects but it took me a long time to work out exactly how I'd apply it in English. English AST, Lisa Jane Ashes has been an invaluable guide here and reading her 'Shakespeare introduction to SOLO'[1] was a light bulb moment.

English teachers often find themselves asking abstract questions like, 'Has Shakespeare influenced all modern writers?' Predictably, we get responses along the lines of, 'No, but he wrote a lot of plays.' Students tend to approach this kind of big picture question with a disappointing lack of engagement, going for the briefest possible answer. After grasping SOLO, they begin to think more carefully about their answers.

It's important to ask questions that are accessible, but at the same time abstract enough to allow pupils to develop their

---

1. http://lisajaneashes.edublogs.org/2012/01/07/introducing-solo-in-english/.

answer to extended abstract questions as the lesson progresses. This is an almost impossible balancing act, so instead, ask a series of questions building up to your big abstract question:

- Who is Shakespeare? (identifying)
- What did he do and why? (describing)
- How does Shakespeare compare to a modern playwright? (analysis)
- Did Shakespeare write every story ever written? (hypothesis)

Try using visual question prompts as a way to reveal and build on each level of thinking:

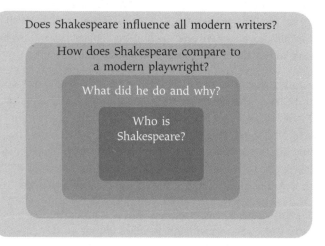

After getting students to spill out everything they know about Shakespeare, you can then add to that knowledge to create a firm multi-structural base from which to proceed.

Gathering multi-structural knowledge about a topic is essential if you're going to further analyse it. Students need to see the relationships between the text that they're studying and its context. One of the assessment objectives for English Literature is that students need to relate texts to their social, cultural and historical background. Without the multi-structural base, students aren't going to be able to make links and are instead stuck with regurgitating the meagre facts we've stuffed into them.

So, with the contextual knowledge secure, you can give out a short extract from a Shakespeare play and an extract from a modern text with influences from Shakespeare (which is virtually anything written in the past four centuries). When students then need to compare the texts they should have no trouble seeing the differences between the present day and Shakespeare's context. This will help them to see connections and will hopefully trigger speculation about why these links exist.

Getting to the final stage of extended abstract is 'rare and takes a great deal of time and effort to attain.'[2] Get students to ask questions about their relational ideas in order to answer the original question: 'Does Shakespeare influence all

2. Geoff Petty, *Evidence Based Teaching*, p. 19.

modern writers?' The sort of extended abstract response we're looking for might be along the lines of:

- Do we see Shakespeare in everything we read because he wrote about such a range of ideas?
- Did Shakespeare write every possible genre of story?
- Are modern writers left with nothing new to write about because Shakespeare got there first?
- Are Shakespeare's stories more important than his use of language?

These questions will enable them to explore ideas about Shakespeare's influence using their excellent relational knowledge to hypothesise creatively about possible answers.

Originality doesn't just happen. Students need to put the spadework in if they are going to come up with something new and interesting. Each of the SOLO stages needs to be completed before moving on to the next. Becoming 'extended abstract' in our thinking is a result of becoming expert enough on a topic to hypothesise about it with evidence and experience.

Recommended Reading

Books

Beadle, Phil, *Could Do Better! Help Your Kid Shine At School* (Doubleday, 2007).

Beadle, Phil, *How To Teach* (Crown House Publishing, 2010).

Beadle, Phil, *Dancing about Architecture: A Little Book of Creativity* (Crown House Publishing, 2011).

Beere, Jackie, *The Perfect Ofsted Lesson* (Crown House Publishing, 2010).

Biggs, John and Collis, Kelvin, *Evaluating the Quality of Learning: The SOLO Taxonomy* (Academic Press, 1982).

Black, Paul and Wiliam, Dylan, *Inside the Black Box: Raising Standards through Classroom Assessment* (NFER Nelson, 1998).

Dweck, Carol, *Mindset: The Psychology of Success* (Ballantine, 2006).

Gilbert, Ian, *Essential Motivation in the Classroom* (Routledge Falmer, 2002).

Recommended Reading

Gilbert, Ian, *Why Do I Need a Teacher When I've Got Google?* (Routledge, 2011).

Gladwell, Malcolm, *Outliers: The Story of Success* (Penguin, 2009).

Godin, Seth, *Linchpin: How to be Indispensible* (Piatkus, 2010).

Hattie, John, *Visible Learning: A Synthesis of Over 800 Meta-Analyses Relating to Achievement* (Routledge, 2009).

Hattie, John, *Visible Learning for Teachers* (Routledge, 2012).

Hirsch, E. D., *The Knowledge Deficit: Closing the Shocking Education Gap for American Children* (Houghton Mifflin Harcourt, 2007).

Hook, Pam and Mills, Julie, *SOLO Taxonomy: A Guide for Schools. Book 1: A Common Language of Learning* (Essential Resources, 2012).

Martin, Steve, *Using SOLO as a Framework for Teaching: A Case Study in Maximising Achievement in Science* (Essential Resources, 2011).

Nuthall, Graham, *The Hidden Lives of Learners* (NZCER Press, 2007).

Ofsted, *Generic Grade Descriptors and Supplementary Subject-Specific Guidance for Inspectors on Making Judgements during Subject Survey Visits to Schools* (1 January 2012). Ref. 20100015. Available at http://www.ofsted.gov.uk/resources/generic-grade-descriptors-and-supplementary-subject-specific-guidance-for-inspectors-making-judgemen/ (accessed 18 April 2012).

Ofsted, *Moving English Forward: Action to Raise Standards in English* (15 March 2012). Ref: 110118. Available at http://www.ofsted.gov.uk/resources/moving-english-forward/ (accessed 18 April 2012).

Ofsted, *The Evaluation Schedule for the Inspection of Maintained Schools and Academies from January 2012* (30 March 2012). Ref. 090098. Available at http://www.ofsted.gov.uk/resources/evaluation-schedule-for-inspection-of-maintained-schools-and-academies-january-2012/ (accessed 18 April 2012).

Paton, Graeme, 'Michael Gove: Pupils Should Read 50 Books a Year', *Daily Telegraph*, 22 March 2011. Available at http://www.telegraph.co.uk/education/educationnews/8396823/Michael-Gove-pupils-should-read-50-books-a-year.html/. (accessed 18 April 2012).

Petty, Geoff, *Evidence-Based Teaching: A Practical Approach*, 2nd edn (Nelson Thornes, 2009).

Reeves, Douglas (ed.), *Ahead of the Curve: The Power of Assessment to Transform Teaching and Learning* (Solution Tree Press, 2007).

Robinson, Ken and Aronica, Lou, *The Element: How Finding Your Passion Changes Everything* (Penguin, 2010).

Rothstein, Dan and Santana, Luz, 'Teaching Students to Ask Their Own Questions: One Small Change Can Yield Big

Results', *Harvard Education Letter* 27(5) (2011). Available at http://www.hepg.org/hel/article/507/ (accessed 18 April 2012).

Smith, Alistair, *High Performers: The Secrets of Successful Schools* (Crown House Publishing, 2011).

Syed, Matthew, *Bounce: The Myth of Talent and the Power of Practice* (Fourth Estate, 2011).

Wiliam, Dylan, *Assessment for Learning: Why, What and How?* (Institute of Education, University of London, 2009).

Willingham, Daniel, *Why Don't Students Like School?* (Wiley, 2009).

Wiseman, Richard, *59 Seconds: Think a Little, Change a Lot* (Pan Books, 2010).

Wright, Trevor, *How to be a Brilliant English Teacher* (Routledge, 2005).

Blogs

Ashes, Lisa Jane, *Reflections of a Learning Geek* – lisajaneashes.edublogs.org

Bennett, Tom, *The Behaviour Guru* – behaviourguru.blogspot.com

Clark, Damian, *In Visible Learning* – invisiblelearning.blogspot.co.uk

Recommended Reading

Coles, Tait, *Taitcoles* – taitcoles.wordpress.com

Didau, David, *The Learning Spy* – learningspy.co.uk

Elder, Zoë, *Full-On Learning* – www.fullonlearning.com

Evans, Mark, *Teach It So* – www.teachit.so

Gilbert, Ian, *Independent Thinking* – independentthinking.posterous.com

Mead, Darren, *Pedagogical Purposes* – pedagogicalpurposes.blogspot.com

Michie James – jamesmichie.com

Pieper, Kenny, *Just Trying To Be Better Than Yesterday* – justtryingtobebetter.wordpress.com

Old, Andrew, *Scenes from the Battleground* – teachingbattleground.wordpress.com

Still, Kristian, *Kristian Still's Blog* – www.kristianstill.co.uk/wordpress

Sutherland, Laura, *300000 Questions* – 300000questions.wordpress.com

The Perfect Series

The Perfect (Ofsted) Lesson by Jackie Beere
edited by Ian Gilbert ISBN 978-1-84590-460-9

The Perfect (Ofsted) Inspection by Jackie Beere
edited by Ian Gilbert ISBN 978-1-78135-000-3

The Perfect (Ofsted) English Lesson by David Didau
edited by Jackie Beere ISBN 978-1-78135-052-2

The Perfect (Teacher) Coach
by Terri Broughton edited by Jackie Beere
ISBN 978-1-78135-003-4

Perfect Assessment (for Learning) by Claire Gadsby
edited by Jackie Beere ISBN 978-1-78135-002-7

 Bringing together some of the most innovative practitioners working
in education today under the guidance of Ian Gilbert, founder of
Independent Thinking Ltd. www.independentthinkingpress.com